D0758203

His, Mine, and Ours

His, Mine, and Ours

A GUIDE TO KEEPING MARRIAGE FROM RUINING A PERFECTLY GOOD RELATIONSHIP

Anne Seifert

Macmillan Publishing Co., Inc.

Macmillan Publishing Co., Inc.
866 Third Avenue, New York, N.Y. 10022
Collier Macmillan Canada, Ltd.

Library of Congress Cataloging in Publication Data

Seifert, Anne.
　　His, mine, and ours.

　　Includes bibliographical references.
　　1. Marriage. 2. Marriage—United States.
I. Title.
HQ734.S463 301.42 79-13186
ISBN 0-02-609030-9

First Printing 1979

Printed in the United States of America

　　Excerpts from "Doin' What Comes Natur'lly" by Irving
Berlin at top of Chapter 3, page 22, and at top of Chapter 7,
page 73, © Copyright 1946, Irving Berlin. Reprinted by
Permission of Irving Berlin Music Corporation.
　　Excerpts from "Oklahoma!" by Richard Rodgers and
Oscar Hammerstein II following chapter titles on pp. 3,
14, 39, 53, 61, 88, 104, 113, 131, 146, 155, and 170 ©
Copyright 1943 by Williamson Music, Inc.

To Fred

Contents

PART II LOSING YOUR IDENTITY, INDEPENDENCE, AND FREEDOM

PART III REGAINING YOUR IDENTITY, INDEPENDENCE, AND FREEDOM

PART IV   FINDING SOLUTIONS

PART V   STARTING FROM HOME BASE

Acknowledgments

WRITING THIS BOOK might have been a lonely experience except that some very special people lent encouragement and assistance.

Horace Schwartz of the Writer's Bookstore introduced the world of publishing and patiently taught the rules of the game. Pat Montandon guided me along the path of authorship. Her warmth and understanding assured each step. Paul Erdman appeared when the going got tough, boosted my spirits, and came to my aid.

My friends inspired, consoled, advised, shared ideas, and waded through the rough drafts. Ralph Gainey humored, cajoled, and played a welcome role as devil's advocate. Jane McEwen, Layle and Jack Luckett, Joan Ullyot, Bae Emilson, Judith B. Henderson, Grace Richardson, Elbrun Revere Kimmelman, Carlene Hatchell Clarke, Susan Smith Armstrong, and Grace and Barbara Morr provided a steady flow of empathetic support. My parents, aunt Adele, and sister Louise labored over the first draft and critiqued with love. Shirley Radl and Covert Bailey counselled. My husband gave me hugs.

Diane Kirsten-Martin mercilessly criticized my ideas and written expression. Through her sharp observations, however, I gained invaluable training as a writer.

Lynn Garnica applied her talented hand to the illustrations. Elvira Jolan Orly offered legal insight.

Joanie Wheeler Redington added the finishing touches. She proofread, made editorial corrections, and typed the final manuscript. Moreover, Joanie doled out large doses of moral support.

I am especially pleased that Elisabeth Scharlatt is my editor at Macmillan, for which I owe my agent, Julian Bach, a debt of gratitude. She created the winning title and turned worn manuscript pages into a polished book.

Others, not mentioned here, expressed interest in different ways. They volunteered, "I know something you should add to the book." They asked, "How is the book coming?"

It's here! Thank you all.

ANNE SEIFERT
San Francisco, California
December 1978

Part I

Marching to the Altar

CHAPTER **1**

Restructuring Relationships

"It ain't too early and it ain't too late. . . ."

SOMETHING, IT SEEMS, is terribly wrong with marriage.

Fewer people are getting married, and those who do, marry later in life. Married couples are planning to have fewer children than preceding generations or choose to have none at all. Marriage and remarriage rates are declining while divorce rates soar.*

Studies on happiness show that single women are happier than single men. Married women may say they are happy, but they are apt to be more passive, more phobic, and more depressed than married men.** More and more individuals

---

* Jean Lipman-Blumen, "Demographic Trends and Issues in Women's Health." Paper delivered at the Women and Health Conference, San Francisco, Calif., 1975.

** Norman Bradburn, *The Structure of Psychological Well-Being* (Chicago: Aldine Publishing Co., 1969), pp. 148–149; and Jean Callahan, "Why Are All Marriages Breaking Up?" *Mother Jones*, vol. 2, no. 6 (July 1977), p. 22.

seek alternatives. Is marriage, as we know it, behind the times?

When I married I was faced with many of the problems couples struggle with today. With raised expectations and ambitions nurtured by the women's movement, I sensed the need to tailor my marriage to fit my ideals.

At the time we were like any other couple on the marriage path. Berkeley was where we met, amidst the turmoil of the sixties (the People's Park-Vietnam-"tear-it-down"-"burn-it-up" years). I was a student in public health; he was a student in business administration. In appearance and attitude we could easily be overlooked on a campus of budding radicals. He was recently back from a tour of duty in Vietnam, and I, always left of center, could not resist the attraction of opposites. The courtship was traditional; the marriage would be (although I had no definite plans) anything but.

One weekend, to the shock and chagrin of both sets of parents, we drove to Reno, Nevada, and married. Neither of us anticipated the changes in our life that would follow. My husband, expecting the traditional marriage, was unprepared for my reaction.

My world changed. I was a *married* woman. To my professors, this implied the end of my career. To my parents, this meant they would have grandchildren. To others, I was a housewife. To me, it meant only that I would share my life with someone else. But overnight I had lost status.

I lost my financial independence. Charge accounts went into my husband's name. My stockbroker now bought and sold shares for my husband (I was only the messenger).

I lost the name I had for twenty-six years.

I lost my free time, which was now occupied with endless housework. I lost, it seemed, my self.

In spite of this shock, I continued my studies in public health while my husband assaulted the world with his newly acquired business acumen. The adjustment for two people, both single for twenty-six years, was tremendous. We loved each other. We cared. Yet the marriage was far from ideal. At one point, I was sure we would divorce before the year was out.

My consciousness was raised and I was married! I had three alternatives: to accept and learn to enjoy the chains of matrimony, to fight for independence within marriage, or to file for divorce.

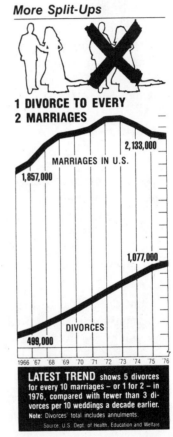

More Split-Ups

1 DIVORCE TO EVERY 2 MARRIAGES

2,133,000

MARRIAGES IN U.S.

1,857,000

1,077,000

DIVORCES

499,000

1966 '67 '68 '69 '70 '71 '72 '73 '74 '75 '76

LATEST TREND shows 5 divorces for every 10 marriages – or 1 for 2 – in 1976, compared with fewer than 3 divorces per 10 weddings a decade earlier.

Note: Divorces' total includes annulments.

Source: U.S. Dept. of Health, Education and Welfare

To complicate matters, we discovered we had totally different tastes. I loved art shows. He loved motorcycle races. I liked old wood houses. He liked new modern houses. I wanted a Chevrolet. He wanted a Porsche. Philosophy was my interest. Machines were his. I loved to listen to Baroque ensembles. He rocked to Linda Ronstadt.

The third alternative, the prospect of divorce, loomed larger. But, I reasoned, if we loved each other, there should be a way to make the marriage work. Strangely, the public health research skills I learned in my studies became valuable tools for analyzing our marriage. Two circumstances combined at the same time—my ability to analyze a problem using a researcher's eye, and marriage in the wake of an emerging women's movement. I chose to fight for my independence in marriage.

Marriage Mechanics

Marriage, the institution, *is* failing to meet the needs of couples. Today, every young married is a pioneer. There are no maps, no guidelines to show anyone the way to a happy, successful life combining one or more careers with marriage. You are on your own. But the results of coping with the demands of modern life with antiquated forms of marriage can be devastating.

The women I knew as undergraduates in college were alert, brilliant, inquisitive, and assured. When I met these same women accompanied by their husbands at an alumnae function ten years later, not one asked a question of the guest speaker; they all sat mute while their husbands spoke for them.

This phenomenon is viewed by Jessie Bernard as Public Health Problem Number One:

If we were in fact epidemiologists and we saw bright, promising young people enter a certain occupation and little by little begin to droop and finally succumb, we would be alerted at once and bend all our research efforts to locate the hazards and remove them. But we are complacent when we see what happens to women in marriage. We put an enormous premium on their getting married, but make them pay an unconscionable price for falling in with our expectations.*

In analyzing my own marriage much as a public-health researcher would analyze a health problem, I recalled that most public health advances were made, not by destroying the agent of disease or identifying host factors (the characteristics of susceptible people), but by changing environmental factors. Disease prevention can be accomplished by intervening on any one of these three levels. However, simple environmental improvements (such as better sanitation and nutrition) have generally relieved most of the world of widespread disease.

If the marriage institution contributes to the breakdown of a relationship, could we also cure *this* syndrome by attacking the problem on a structural level? Most marriage manuals tend to neglect the environmental or structural influences of the institution of marriage on relationships and concentrate instead on the agent of distress (your psychological problems) or personal characteristics (you're too fat, too short, too boring). Psychological and physical self-improvement approaches can work because they are interventions that may reverse the breakdown process, but they may also involve a cost—sacrifice of the self.

Marriage comprises a system of relationships that work when all components are balanced. The system can be depicted as follows:

* Jessie Bernard, "Marriage: Hers and His," *Ms.*, vol. 1, no. 6 (December 1972), p. 113.

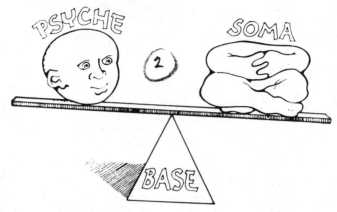

PERFECT HARMONY

When the psychological (psyche) and physical (soma) interactions are in balance with the structure of the relationship (base), there is perfect harmony. An imbalance can occur when there is too much or too little psyche or soma, or the wrong base. For example, if a big ego overpowers the marital relationship, the harmony would be upset:

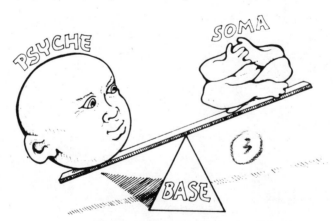

BIG EGO PROBLEM

Or, if passion overrules reason:

SEX PROBLEM

To restore the relationship to perfect harmony when the basic structure of the relationship is fixed, we could reduce the psyche to correct for Big Ego or, in the second case, decrease the soma to correct for Sex Problem. The easiest solution, however, is not to change psyche or soma but to change the position of the base—the structure of your relationship—to meet psyche and soma needs.

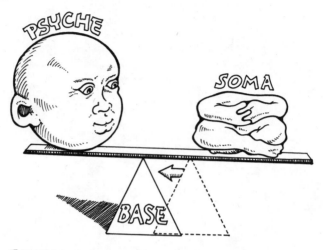

CORRECTED **BIG EGO PROBLEM**

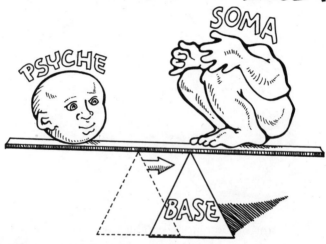

CORRECTED **SEX PROBLEM**

The notion of six years of psychoanalysis to change myself, and the idea of bleaching my hair, wearing a black negli-
gee, or putting love notes in my husband's lunch pail to
"spice up" my marriage were unappealing to me. Instead, fol-

lowing the public health approach, I sought to change the marriage environment.

This book is not a guide for self-counselling or psycho-analysis (hang on to your hang-ups). Nor is it a manual for putting lust in your life (keep your old flannel pajamas). You will learn how to improve your marital happiness, not by altering yourself, but by changing the structure of your marriage.

From my own experience and my observation of married couples and even couples who "live together," I have discovered that confusion, unhappiness, and mistrust often arise as a direct result of a fixed married role model. This book is not for or against marriage, but it will alert you to the pitfalls of marriage and provide new ways to restructure your relationship. Almost any two people can get along (assuming there is a basic and earnest emotional attachment) if they follow the principles illustrated in this book. And I don't mean *just* get along, but become, and stay, excited about their partners and their lives together.

Four Structural Stressors

Marriage problems, as identified by marriage counsellors, usually concern money, sexual incompatibility, child-raising, the uses of leisure time, in-law relationships, and the division of household and family responsibilities. To this list I have added problems of identity and privacy.

Solutions can be approached for many of these dilemmas by analyzing the structure of four major marital stressors: identity, money, housework, and space. Working from this analysis, this book maps out specific techniques of change to restructure your relationship along new lines.

Women, the nurturers, often feel a greater responsibility than men for the success or failure of their marriage. A married woman can become a mother to her husband as well as to her children. But a husband shares the responsibility for the marriage and should not be treated like a child.

Similarly, a husband should not undermine the ability of a woman to stand on her own two feet—she is not a child, either. Both are adults capable of equal partnership. Personal satisfactions will be reflected in their relationship. This book is directed to women, not to encourage responsibility for marital success, but to promote responsibility for their personal happiness by evaluating the structure of their marriages to determine if they contribute to happiness.

My husband and I have developed arrangements to correct a marriage that suffered from traditional structural assumptions. A man who attended an eastern men's college, who was a naval officer for four years, and who earned a masters in business administration is the man I married. At one time or another he has argued against every innovation in this book. I didn't marry a naturally liberal or revolutionary man. With love at the base, though, he was willing to try new ideas and I was willing to look for alternatives. I cannot guarantee our solutions will work for you, but they have worked for one woman and one man.

There is, in all probability, nothing wrong with you or your partner. But there is something wrong with marriage's present rigid structure. Happiness in marriage (as in life) is self-defined. For most people it includes a feeling of elation, of love for yourself and others, and the continuing desire to share your life with another.

Anything that stands in the way of these goals should, logically, be changed or be removed. The chapters ahead will discuss the origins of marriage; provide technical solutions to identity, money, housework, and space inequities; guide you in the art of negotiation; and outline general principles to follow on the marital journey.

The social institution of marriage does not have to be oppressive and devastating to the individual. We are granted both the burden and the opportunity to tap a freedom and happiness in our relationships.

Anyone can be married—the challenge is to be *happily* married, to direct and shape your marriage into a vehicle that carries you toward your desires and goals. It is not a given shape into which you must contort your souls.

This book is for women and men who want it all—love, happiness, and freedom.

If that is you, read on.

CHAPTER **2**

A Perspective:
Here Comes the Bride

"I knowed whut's right and wrong since I been ten. . . ."

MARRIED STATUS IS CHAMPIONED IN A SOCIETY that places great premium on the family group. Love or the inability "to live without it" lies at the structural base of most marriages. However, marriage is not a logical consequence of love, and in some societies, love and marriage are totally unrelated —in which case marriage can be antecedent to love. The framework of marriage is constantly changing over time, adapting to societies' priorities.

In historical perspective, the institution of marriage is a relatively new development. No one knows exactly how it started. In the cave, men and women probably cohabited without formal obligation.

Social institutions originate in the interest of group survi-

14

val. Following this premise, early man and woman must have united for mutual benefit. The facts specific to gender undoubtedly played a role. The male of the species, because of his greater muscular strength, became a hunter and warrior, capable of forcing anyone weaker under his control. The female was vulnerable to force, but capable of bearing children and better equipped physiologically to withstand stress. She probably relied on the physical strength of man to protect her from danger (and other men) and to care for her when she was with child.

Edward Westermarck theorizes, in *A Short History of Marriage*,* that wedlock originally came about as a result of the need for protection of the newborn child. In my view, women, especially vulnerable during pregnancy and child-rearing, called men into service to protect them. Men responded and discovered advantages in doing so. The male became the wooer. The female exercised choice. As part of the bargain, early man exacted services in exchange. He may have said in essence, "I will be happy to protect you and provide for you as long as you will do some work."

Early cave dwellers, it is believed, were basically monogamous. Man, the species, preferred one spouse, probably for economic as well as romantic reasons. Even when more than one spouse was available, one spouse was dominant in affection and favors. The others became the servants or laborers of the house. George Elliott Howard, in his fascinating book, *A History of Matrimonial Institutions*,** states that sexual communism as a primitive and general phase of life is inconsistent with the biological, economic, and psychological laws which determine the general course of organic evolution.

Primitive monogamy contributed to survival of the species. The origins of marriage developed from these primitive relationships. One man and one woman identified themselves as

* New York: Humanities Press, Inc., 1968.
** Chicago: University of Chicago Press, 1904.

belonging together. Gradually, what could be called marriage, a recognized union, emerged. Pairing, with the mutual consent of both parties, was the typical and most popular form of marriage, although other forms (polygyny, polyandry) coexisted and were tolerated.

The wheel was invented. Tools were discovered. Man began to control his environment. Some societies advanced more than others, technologically and socially.

This description of Babylonian marriage may come as a surprise to the twentieth-century women still fighting for equal rights:

At times it would seem as if we must pronounce the Babylonian family to have been patriarchal in character; at other times the wife and mother occupies an independent and even commanding position. It may be noted that whereas in the old Sumerian hymns the woman takes precedence over the man, Semitic translation invariably reverses the order: the one has "female and male," the other "male and female." (*Babylonians and Assyrians*, 13.) The practical result was that the sexes were nearly equal in marriage. The individual and not the family was the social unit and the individuality of the woman was fully recognized. She controlled her own property. She could buy and sell, borrow and lend, sue and be sued and inherit equally with her brother. She might become a priestess, the head of a city or queen of the state. The wife was the husband's equal in the business world. The possession of property "brought with it the enjoyment of considerable authority." She "could act apart from her husband, could enter into partnership, could trade with her money and conduct lawsuits in her own name." (*Idem*, "Social Life Among the Assyrians and Babylonians," 50, 51.)

. . . The bride's dower was paid by her father to the bridegroom but it was her property. Sometimes the husband enjoyed the use of it for life, sometimes the wife disposed of it as her private capital. It was always a means of securing her economic independence and thus of promoting the happiness of her married life. "In this she was protected from tyrannical conduct upon his part as well as from the fear of divorce on insufficient grounds. If a divorce took place, the husband was requested to hand over to the wife all the property she brought with her as dowry; she then either returned to her father's home or set up an independent establishment of her own." The divorced woman might marry again if she chose. "Marriage was partly a religious and partly a civil function. The contracting parties consequently invited the gods and signed the contract in the presence of the priest; at the same time it was a contract and in order to be legally valid it had to be dressed up in legal form and attested by a number of witnesses." (*Ibid.*) *

With a change in economic circumstances and the recognition of real property, new marriage structures appeared. To the downfall of woman, her services were valued. As men became more "civilized" and gained the right to ownership, two forms of marriage, previously unknown, appeared—marriage by capture superseded by marriage by purchase. Mutual consent of the parties was no longer needed. Individual inclinations were not considered. Woman's liberty suffered. Purchased for their services, women were given (by husband or father "protector") in exchange for property. The price paid was not only for the loss of service to the father but for the right of the protectorship. The right was transferred upon purchase from father to husband. Chastity affected the bridal price.

The female surrendered her freedom and virgin purity out of fear of the physically stronger and violent male. The wife-purchase custom offended the feelings and dignity of women. (In some countries today, a bride price is still paid to the father for loss of the daughter's services.) Women, once partners by consent, were now chattel.

Families, concerned about the well-being of their daughters, offered them to suitable mates (usually of greater wealth or standing), adding a cow or a goat to make the offer more attractive; hence the advent of the dowry. Details of this cus-

* Howard, *Matrimonial Institutions*, pp. 221–222.

tom varied. Nevertheless, a woman was a commodity with which one could barter.

Woman as property also limited the freedom of man. Women were safeguarded by their fathers and husbands from other men. Marriage by capture arose when men too poor or unable to procure a wife in the usual way resorted to wife-stealing. During war, women were confiscated to serve as slaves and represented trophies of conquest.

Although services traditionally provided by women were and continue to be valuable to men, generally the trend toward female subjugation is being halted.

From the beginning in the cave, an exchange of services was based on economic necessity and survival. Those women able to strike a good bargain survived; those men able to protect and care for their mates had children. Survival of the species was dependent upon this relationship. Pairing has probably endured because this basic economic dependency is so deeply rooted in our struggle for existence.

But men were in a better position to bargain. Women were truly dependent on male protection. The vestiges of this dependency remain with us today. In a technological society, however, where brains are more powerful than brawn and where women are able to control reproduction as well as develop their skills in the marketplace, women are now able to strike a better bargain.

Custom, Ceremony, and Law

Remnants of old marriage customs are symbolized in today's ceremonies and traditions. For example, wife-capture is mocked by the playful act of carrying the bride across the threshold. The father "gives away" the bride. White symbolizes her virtue.

Local custom dictated the form and ritual of marriage. Publicity was the crucial element for validating the marriage and for distinguishing it from an illicit union. This created the pageantry and hoopla we associate with the marriage ceremony. Tokens, such as rings, also served to publicize the union.

Looking at the development of marriage in England prior to the tenth century, we find that there was no religious doctrine concerning marriage. The church accepted local custom, but religious benediction was unessential to legitimize marriage. As church membership increased and the religious aspect of marriage gained popularity, however, more couples desired God's blessing on their new union. The newly wed couple proceeded to the church for religious services.

Two marriage ceremonies evolved—one dictated by local custom and the other by the seeking of holy grace. Church ceremonies, usually performed on the steps, moved inside. Between the tenth and twelfth centuries an elaborate marriage ritual developed, with the priest directing the entire celebration. One century later, the priest could substitute for the bride's father. The clergy appropriated this function as their exclusive right. The consequence: whereas previously only private contract and mutual consent were necessary for marriage, religious sanction was now needed. The Protestant Reformation brought with it the doctrine of Luther. Marriage (unless unconsummated) was indissoluble. In 1563, the Council of Trent declared invalid any marriage not performed by a priest.

Matrimonial law developed and was administered by celibate Christian Fathers who viewed marriage as a compromise between man and lust. Women, regarded as embodying sexual temptation, were despised. Intercourse was considered a necessary evil even within marriage, except for purposes of procreation.

Ironically, the church failed miserably as an administrator of marriage law. The clergy regarded itself as holier than the general populace because its members were celibate and did not yield to the temptations of marriage. The church made conjugal infidelity by the husband equally sinful with that of the wife. Marriage was a sacrament. As such, marriages could not be dissolved and the church assumed jurisdiction over matrimonial matters. All those unable to bear the superior state of virginity were urged to marry. Requirements for parental consent were abandoned and child marriages condoned. Abuses, misuses, and exploitation of individuals resulted. To evade religious authority, secret marriages took place.

The best interests of society were not being served. Any threat against an institution designed to promote group survival could expect to be corrected by social action. The state intervened. To alleviate the miserable conditions rampant under church rule, marital offenses (child abuse, bribery, desertion, bigamy) were placed in the hands of the justice of the peace. Offenders were tried. The state succeeded, in some measure, where the church had failed.

The "Statute of 1753" in England required the celebration of marriage after publication of banns or license. Marriage became a simple, but legal, contract.

Love in Marriage

Love, a strong, sometimes passionate affection for another person, is not the same as marriage. Marriage is the institution whereby men and women are joined in a special kind of social and legal dependence for the purpose of founding and maintaining a family. Most important, marriage is a legal contract and neither the actual nor implied terms are read.

This legal relationship assumes an agreement among you, your mate, the state in which you live, and the federal government to abide by marriage law. But terms of this written and unwritten law are often discovered too late—upon divorce.

It cannot be overemphasized that love and marriage are distinct and separate entities. Only recently, in historical terms (since the eighteenth-century Enlightenment), has the concept of romantic love become prevalent. Love is a feeling, an emotion. Marriage is an event, a ceremony. They should not be confused.

Marriage forms have varied widely throughout time and by geographic region. Twentieth-century marriage, based on mutual consent, is a ceremony enveloped by elaborate ritual and endowed with religious, legal, and social significance. The institution of marriage is here to stay and will continue to shift and alter with society. We are part of the process.

How many of us end up with marriage when what we want is love?

CHAPTER **3**

The Marriage Mill

"Folks are dumb where I come from—they ain't had any learnin'. . . ."

MARRIAGE CAN BE AN UNCHARTED ADVENTURE ruled by chance or a well-planned pursuit. The road to marriage is different for everyone. This journey need not be a mystery for those who have yet to start out on it, and those already at the destination will benefit by recalling the route. Let's look at the process of marriage: Why do people marry? How do they get there?

Growing Up

For most Americans, growing up means struggling for independence from the family. As children in our parents' home, we are secure in a family structure—perhaps not an ideal one, but a structure nonetheless. As we grow older, the

22

need to test ourselves in a world unguarded by well-meaning people intensifies. We want to be on our own, to test life, to become adult. The time comes when self-determination appears possible and, like nestlings, we try our wings. We go to college, into the military, or get a job. Having abandoned the family nest, the return home usually becomes impossible. Rather than revert to children again—a difficult position to bear after sovereignty—we proceed to the Roaming Roommate Experience and the Living Alone Trauma.

THE ROAMING-ROOMMATE EXPERIENCE

With expenses high and income low, the logical thing to do is to team with a roommate, who may be an old friend, a new acquaintance, or a respondent to an ad placed in the local paper. In this acknowledged temporary relationship and living place, careful consideration is given to details concerning rent payment, food-shopping, and bathroom usage; and arrangements are discussed and devised for mutual benefit.

Still, there are failures. My first roommate was someone I'd known in college. We rented a small one-bedroom apartment, and when I returned from a European vacation one summer, I discovered we had a third roommate—her boyfriend. Guess who stayed? I packed my bags and headed for an apartment that I was to share with two other women. Occupying one large bedroom in Cambridge, Massachusetts, were "The Mess," "The Psychoneurotic," and myself—"Nelly Neat Up-Tight." We three nevertheless enjoyed a compatible relationship. When The Psychoneurotic moved out and The Mess went to South America, they were replaced by "I Want to Get Married" and "I'm Engaged." Eventually, I'm Engaged got married, and I Want to Get Married moved back home because she didn't get married. It was my turn. I completed my research work and moved to New York City.

After a while, if roommates become more of a problem than a solution, you may do as I did and decide to live alone.

THE LIVING-ALONE TRAUMA

Living alone is emotionally difficult, hard to sustain, and inclines one toward marriage. Happiness can be achieved in a living-alone situation if you have many friends in the neighborhood, especially one good friend whom you see almost every day. In this kind of atmosphere, single existence can be very pleasant, except for the occasional loss of friends who relocate.

People who require solitude may cherish living alone. Among these are sojourners who have a "mission" to accomplish or a "greater purpose," and those who have others to nurture their egos. Then, of course, there are misanthropes and hermits who genuinely do not like people and are happy only when living alone.

However, for most people, living alone is tough. And if you don't know anyone, living alone can be a horrendous experience. I remember living alone in Boston opposite The Fenway. I knew no one. The only window in my studio apartment framed a gray courtyard, where all I could see was soot falling from the incinerator in a snowflake pattern. Dinner and evenings were spent with television. My bed was a fold-out sofa, with buttons that pushed through the sheets. Meeting new acquaintances and having an occasional date only temporarily relieved the loneliness. The idea of a steady boyfriend looked attractive. The idea of marriage looked better.

When the struggle for freedom and independence has been won, loneliness flowers. Living alone, we seek others. Trying something new, we want to share the adventure with someone else. In this way we discover our human qualities—desire for, and dependence on, the warmth and comfort of others. Increasingly, we are alone as others our age marry. Is marriage the perfect solution?

Nature or Nurture?

Marriage scenarios vary and some people enter marriage directly from the family home, thereby avoiding the Roaming Roommate Experience and the Living Alone Trauma. The marriage impetus is strong. Those who remain single encounter considerable social pressure to marry. The desire to be married is the single person's first step toward reentry into family life, that comfortable coexistence enjoyed prior to the flight to independence.

Why do people marry?

Harry Browne, a lover of freedom and author of *How I Found Freedom in an Unfree World*,* says people marry for the following reasons:

1. To enhance a love relationship.
2. To confirm that one has "won" his lover once and for all.
3. To achieve social respectability (such as to prove one's desirability or to satisfy one's desire to be known as the "head of the family").
4. To make sexual intercourse easily accessible.
5. To be financially supported.
6. To avoid loneliness.
7. To guarantee that someone will be around in one's old age.
8. To have children.
9. To escape the need to do something more challenging with one's life.
10. To have a housekeeper.

* New York: Macmillan Publishing Co., Inc., 1973.

W. J. Lederer and D. D. Jackson, in an article,** cite these reasons for people marrying:

1. During courtship, individuals lose most of their judgment.
2. Society encourages marriage.
3. The pressures and maneuvering of parents push their children into premature and careless marriages.
4. Romantic literature, tradition, and movies have given false values which young singles accept as true.
5. Loneliness drives them into marriage.
6. They have an unconscious desire to improve themselves.
7. They are motivated by neuroses.
8. They miss their fathers or mothers and cannot live without a parental symbol.

Another reason is the age-old, hard-to-refuse proposition: take the marriage vows or experience the business end of a shotgun. However, most people marry because they *want* to be married. And marriage is often a solution to a problem.

Ways to the Wedding

Routes to the altar are as varied as the reasons for marriage. Marriage occurs by chance or by plan. Of the many ways to matrimony, only two are discussed here and are characterized as contrasting personalities on opposite ends of a spectrum. At one end is the person who simply stumbles into marriage and at the other end is the person who plots the march.

TWO WAYS—THE STUMBLER'S AND THE PLOTTER'S

Stumblers are men or women who find love and then marry. Plotters are men or women who plan when to marry and then find love. Most Plotters know they can wait because

** "The Eight Myths of Marriage," *New Woman*, vol. 5, no. 5 (September/October 1975), pp. 67–72.

they have already met more than one suitable spouse. The "one and only" for the Stumbler is the "one of many" for the Plotter. The Plotter thinks, "Well, first I want to go to business school. I want to buy a yacht. I want to have a successful career, and then I want to marry."

I knew a Plotter. He asked me to join him on several dates and in checklist fashion evaluated my potential as a mate. My tennis game was lousy and my cooking worse, so I didn't make it to the altar with him (the chemistry between us was missing too). To my amazement, he found the woman he wanted; they married and share a happy and loving life together. I was impressed. Does plotting work? Can anyone arrange romance?

Plotters select an optimal age for marriage. Relationships occurring at the wrong time are either ended or postponed before emotions swell. In the interim, Plotters may date (albeit subconsciously) unsuitable marriage partners or be involved in impossible situations—thus avoiding the temptation to marry. Stumblers do not understand Plotters. If they meet and the match seems perfect, the Stumbler is bewildered when the Plotter-lover says good-bye. For the Plotter, love does not conquer all. Plotters control their romantic lives whereas Stumblers lose control and don't know when to quit.

Stumblers can also be victims on the road to marriage. The best-known and most troublesome obstacle, causing untold grief and wasted years for single men and—seemingly with greater frequency and more devastating results—for single women, is the affair with an already-married lover.

If you're a single woman, a surefire way *not* to get to the altar is with a married man. A married man is already committed. He can be dashing, powerful, romantic, and free with the words you want to hear, but he has enormous leverage in your relationship. Your time together is dictated by your married lover's whims, schedule, and guilt feelings toward the spouse at home—a situation as unfair as it is dishonest.

The lavish attention often bestowed by married men is

hard to resist. I know several women who have waited for married men for five or more years. One woman was twenty-five when she met her lover. She is now thirty. Her lover did get a divorce, but he has to make large alimony payments, and now that he and the woman are on a realistic and equal footing, their emotional life has dwindled. Wait until the divorce papers are signed before you start that affair. If you value your time (like the Plotter), you will not spend it waiting for a married man when you could be spending it with a more suitable and honest beau. You may say second best is better than nothing. But if marriage is a goal for you, accepting second best will keep you off the trail.

YOUR WEDDING WAY

Most married people are neither all-Plotter nor all-Stumbler but possess characteristics of each. A time came when, simultaneously, you were ripe for marriage and the right person arrived. Only you know how you ventured through the marriage mill. To refresh your memory—because you need to know where you've been before you can chart where you're going—try the following two exercises. (If you are not married, the analysis will enlighten future encounters.)

Get a pencil and a piece of paper—or refer to the following Process Work Sheets—and relax in a comfortable chair. The two processes will tell you why you are married and how you got there. Using the Past Living Arrangement process and the Past Romance Relationship process will also help you to discover if you really *want* independence and freedom in marriage.

Past Living-Arrangement Process:

1. Think back to your earliest living situation—as far back as you can remember. Was it at home with your parents?

Recall the physical environment, the people around you, the people close to you, and the city, town, or rural area where you lived.

2. Starting with this earliest recollection, list every one of your living situations from that time to the present. Do not record any living situation—that is, the circumstances and the people around you—until it is clearly pictured in your mind. Now capture the essence of that period with only a few descriptive words so you can easily recall the situation later.

3. Using plus (+) and minus (−) labels, identify the living situations that were happy (+) and unhappy (−) for you. Your first reaction is important, so review the list quickly. Add another plus sign to the *very happy* situations (++) and two more plus signs to the *extremely happy* situations (+++). In similiar fashion, add one minus sign to *very unhappy* situation (− −) or two more minus signs to *extremely unhappy* living situations (− − −).

4. Were your living situations happy? Unhappy? And were some better than others?

   Look at the happy living situations: What kind of relationships did you share with the people around you? Were you dependent on others? Independent?

5. Think about any living situations with roommates: Where are they on your list? Which ones were happy or unhappy? In which situations were living arrangements clearly delineated in the beginning? Were the rules of your arrangement understood? Could you discuss the things you wanted to change? Was there a sincere interest in resolving conflicts? Could you accept each other's differences?

6. Looking at the happy and unhappy situations, what kind of power relationships were present? Who had the most power? In which situations was the power equally distributed?

PROCESS WORK SHEET–PAST LIVING ARRANGEMENTS

Past Living Arrangement	Happy (+) Unhappy (–)	Were you dependent? Independent?	Did you have clear living arrangements?	Could you discuss what you wanted to change?	Was there sincere interest in resolving conflicts?	Could you accept each other's differences?	Who had the most power?
(list)	(rate)	(dep./ind.)	(yes/no)	(yes/no)	(yes/no)	(yes/no)	(me/other)
1.							
2.							
3.							
4.							
5.							
6.							
7.							
8.							
9.							
10.							

NOW:

If you were in a situation with two or more roommates, did two ever side against one? As roommates—one to one—was there equal power? Why was the distribution of power equal or unequal?

Did one roommate pay a larger share of the rent or own most of the furniture?

7. Summarize your findings. Are you in a happy living situation now? Who has the most power? Do you feel independent?

In this simple way, your happiness now can be evaluated and you can gain insight into the ways to make yourself happier. However, we still do not know why you are married. Do you? To complete the analysis, take a different step back in time with the Past Romance-Relationship process. And don't despair if you're not happy now—read on.

With your pencil in hand, begin the second process.

Past Romance-Relationship Process:

1. Recall yourself at sixteen years of age. What were you like? Where were you living? What were the circumstances? Get a good picture of yourself, because we will go forward a year at a time.

2. Starting at sixteen, move through each year until you reach today, and list every emotionally significant romantic experience. (Only you can be the judge of which relationships were significant. If you can't remember them, they're probably not significant.)

3. Using the plus-and-minus label system again, identify the romantic relationships that brought happiness and those that were a constant torment. Don't base your evaluations on how they ended, only on how they were overall during the courtship. What was the special quality of the relationship?

PROCESS WORK SHEET–PAST ROMANCE RELATIONSHIPS

Significant Romances	Happy (+) Unhappy (–)	Who was most power-ful?	Was there an equal partnership?	Did you feel loved?	How did you feel?	How were you treated?	How did you react?
(list)	(rate)	(me/other)	(yes/no)	(yes/no)	(lousy/great)	(good/bad)	(glad/hurt)
1.							
2.							
3.							
4.							
5.							
6.							
7.							
8.							
9.							
10.							

NOW:

4. Which were the happy romances? Which were the sad affairs? Who was most powerful in the relationship? Were there any equal partnerships? Did you feel loved? How *did* you feel?

5. Looking at your happy romances, see if you can discover why they were happy. How were you treated? How did you react?

6. Dwell on these questions and answer them to your own satisfaction. Are you happy now? Is feeling independent important to you? Do you have a good relationship, one that brings you happiness now?

What do the answers to these questions mean for your future happiness? If they indicate that independence and freedom are linked to your happiness, you will be able to achieve that state again *within* your marriage by following the suggestions in this book. Use this simple rule of thumb: Does single life look much more attractive to you than your married life? If the answer is "yes," then you should either revitalize your marriage or become single again. But don't rush to the divorce court! If you were single again, you might both be attracted to one another as before and marriage might again destroy the harmony. The answer may *not* be another person. The answer may be another type of marriage with the same person.

Now That You're Married

Few married persons analyze the fine print of their assumed marriage contract. Blithely, couples walk hand in hand to a wedding march never suspecting that married status can have negative ramifications.

Basic assumptions about married people prevail in our culture. These assumptions are reflected in law and in stereotypic portrayals of married life. Since marriage is often the solution to a problem, and the reason for and the route to marriage are different for everyone, how could life after marriage be the *same* for everyone? It isn't. A marriage based on false assumptions is a marriage based on unsound foundations.

THE BLESSED ASSUMPTIONS

Blessed Assumptions (made in Heaven) permeate every fiber of married life and dictate role relationships between wife and husband.

Commonly accepted assumptions about married people:

1. They are a male and female.
2. The union is limited to two people.
3. They married to have a family.
4. The husband is the sole provider of income.
5. The wife attends to the needs of husband and children.
6. The husband, as provider, willingly supports wife and children.
7. The wife is dependent on the husband's income.
8. The wife is somehow inferior to her husband but also "the better half."
9. They are married forever and . . .
10. Two people are one—the husband!

Assumptions 1 and 2 are generally true, but even these accepted statements do not apply to all married people. Same-sex marriages are gaining acceptance. Certain religious sects, especially in pioneer days, approved group marriage.

Numbers 3 and 4 are not always true. Today's couples frequently postpone the decision to have children or marry to maintain a love companionship with no intention of ever having children. Also, fewer couples expect to be supported by one paycheck.

In some households, assumptions 5 through 8 may hold

true, but not for women with unemployed husbands, or women with careers or their own income (48 percent of all American women are in the labor force).

Sorry, but marriage is not always "forever," as stated in assumption 9. Contrary to assumption 10, two people are definitely not one—the laws of physics defy it. However, psychologically and legally, in marriage, it is supposedly possible.

Acceptance of these Blessed Assumptions can ruin a potentially good marital relationship. These role assumptions have evolved over time in response to economic circumstances and generally will work; but many things that work are not optimally desirable. Marriage based on assumptions can result in a workable living arrangement, but it may not be geared to maximize *your* personal happiness.

Being married is like learning to ski. At first you see the steep slopes, the potential problems in negotiating turns, and then one day, the slopes are conquered, the moguls mastered. You are comfortable, there is little risk of injury, and you actually start to enjoy the scenery.

Once you have established a working relationship with your partner, married life can be happier on the whole than single life ever was. You may experience fewer thrills—the highs and lows of single life—but you can now enjoy the ride.

In marriage you can consolidate both your physical and emotional energies with your mate. You expect the relationship to continue. But a major disadvantage of marriage is your acceptance of the cultural expectations of the husband-wife roles. And in some states, there are still significant legal barriers based on sex-role that will limit your freedom. Also, because of the usual depth of commitment in marriage, there is greater emotional risk than might otherwise be present in a relationship. However, the reward of happiness ever after is well worth the effort required to learn how to negotiate the marriage moguls. Think of all the happy expert skiers.

A healthy person stands on his own two feet, not making undue demands or impositions on others. He is capable of creative adjustment as well as conformity to the symbols and expectations of his culture. He can accept or reject alternatives and make important decisions and carry them out. He has a well-developed inner life and alternates solitude and meditation with creative activities and social life so that he is not cut off from his fellow man but can share his life with others with love, tenderness and compassion.*

The marriage process begins in our parents' home. Struggling for freedom and happiness, we discover marriage is the missing piece in the happiness puzzle. Everyone approaches the solution in a different way. Some systematically examine the edges and content of the puzzle before finding the clincher. Others stumble upon the correctly shaped cutout and solve the problem without further ado.

When you marry, you inherit social expectations. These expectations are based on assumptions about the nature of your relationship. Because these assumptions are confining for people who don't fit precomposed pictures, a new struggle emerges—the search for another marriage picture better suited to your own contours.

* H. S. Hoyman, "Our Modern Concept of Health," *Journal of School Health*, vol. 32, (1962), p. 258.

Part II

Losing Your Identity, Independence, and Freedom

CHAPTER **4**

What's Wrong?

"I heared a lot of stories and I reckon they are true. . . ."

ONE DAY YOU WERE SINGLE; one day you were married. Did you change? Maybe a little, but not much. Did the expectations of others change? Did your own expectations change? The answer is probably yes.

Marriage brings with it role models based on the Blessed Assumptions. The cultural message is clear: A wife should be a dutiful, socially inclined homemaker, and a thoughtful helpmate to her husband. A husband should be a provider, a climber of some success ladder, a responsible man, and the head of the household. This life program is based on our beliefs and attitudes about men and women. We are saddled with others' expectations, and marriage, the institution, is loaded. When you married, you probably didn't realize there was a baggage car on the train.

The Players

If we wanted to insure that two people would not understand one another or be compatible, we would try to make them as different as possible. From birth, we would teach them different values, encourage them to follow dissimilar interests, and would place them in social opposition to one another. Yet when men and women have difficulty understanding one another, are incompatible, and have to struggle to develop a mutually satisfying relationship, we wonder what's wrong. Men and women, raised to accept predigested roles, are expected after marriage to live happily ever after. But they start with the cards stacked against them. The worlds of man and woman differ.

Gender determines social role. One factor—that the female is capable of bearing children—has dictated the course of woman's socialization process.

The female is reared to attain the social qualities deemed desirable for motherhood. Although some women may choose never to have children, and the child-rearing years occupy only a small percentage of the lifetime of those who do, *all* women are trained to be mothers—to be nurturing ministers. The nurturing role is intrinsic to the female experience. In addition to tending children, woman-the-server learns to please man, because ultimately, as childbearer, she is dependent upon him. Growing-up years are spent in preparation for this great onstage, center-front role in the play of life. But I ask you, who wants to be typecast?

To create social and behavioral differences between the sexes, role preparation starts early. Little girls get dolls; little boys get chemistry sets. Biological differences are emphasized and exaggerated, increasingly as one enters adulthood. Men show their muscles; women display their breasts. A trait at birth—true of all caste-ordered societies—determines the course of a person's socialization process and later social status.

A woman is a man with a womb.

A man is a woman without a womb.*

TYPE CASTE

Part of the learning process in developing a sexual identity comes from role-model identification. We identify with what we see. Often stereotyped male and female images appear in our newspapers, television commercials, and on boxes of breakfast cereal. People identify with these images and imitate these stereotypes, consciously or unconsciously. Also, other people treat man and woman differently—according to *their* image of the gender stereotype. This process feeds upon itself.

Men and women are influenced by the expectations created by these stereotypes. A blonde woman, observing that all blonde women portrayed in the media are dumb, starts to think she's supposed to act dumb. She discovers her dumb behavior brings increased male attention. If she has the figure of a Marilyn Monroe and also the brains and inclination to be a nuclear physicist, she would find it difficult to be accepted as a serious candidate for this profession. She might decide it would be easier to conform to others' expectations than to buck the stereotype.

Thus expectations based on stereotypes are destructive and debilitating. Invariably, people try to make others conform to their preconceived images. But people rarely, if ever, ac-

---

* "[Concerning] the origin of the word, *woman* (*womman* appeared in the late thirteenth century)—some have thought that popular fancy connected the word with *womb*, as if the word were *womb-man*. . . ." From W. W. Skeat, *Etymological Dictionary of the English Language* (Oxford: Clarendon Press, 1909).

tually fit these molds. Do you know any smart blondes who act dumb? Or any housewives who pretend they can't fix anything mechanical? Advertising (perhaps inadvertently) has hurt many classes of people by perpetuating one dominant image associated with hair color or gender.

You may wonder how these images could affect anyone. I will cite some examples from firsthand experience:

I left a post with a well-known research scientist in New York City to attend graduate school in California. While in graduate school, I married. Years later, I overheard my ex-employer state that the reason I left the research position was to get married. This conclusion fitted his stereotype of women, even though, in my case, it was not true. Unfortunately, his comment may have disqualified me in the eyes of the listener for future employment and served to reinforce a harmful stereotype.

At a scientific conference, I met a professor whom I had not seen for ten years. Surprised to see me, he exclaimed, "Didn't you get married and have two children?" (I had married, but I had no children.)

My scientific career was, in fact, uninterrupted by my marriage in spite of the fact that I was refused admission to one graduate school because the chairman feared I would marry; once accepted to another school, my seriousness was questioned because I did marry; and since graduation I have been told by employers that I don't need to work because I am married. The notion of a woman pursuing a career uninterrupted by marriage does not conform to prevalent stereotypes of the married woman.

I made note of another blatant example of stereotypical reasoning when I called my stockbroker and was told that she had left the firm "to take care of her family." This explanation didn't sound plausible to me, since she was a dyed-in-the-wool businesswoman, so I asked for a better explanation.

The man to whom I was talking then stated that my stock-broker's family responsibilities had increased and in order to make more money she and her husband were starting their own business. (Her husband also left his firm. I wondered what *his* ex-employer would have said.)

When a physician friend gave birth to her child in a Boston hospital, she completed the information needed for the birth certificate. Since her husband was also a physician, she listed his occupation as well as her own as "physician." The attend-ing nurse, believing the new mother was confused, changed my friend's occupation to "housewife." Later, when my friend received a copy of the birth certificate she noticed her occu-pation had been altered. She quickly informed the hospital of their error. The hospital refused to change the certificate, maintaining that she was both a physician and a housewife. The record was never changed, although to this day she is a practicing physician. This issue was not important enough to make a federal case out of it, but it was sufficiently im-portant to my friend to make her blood boil. And that's what is wrong with stereotypes. We believe all married women are housewives even if they are not. And if they are not house-wives, we prefer to view them as such anyway. (I am always amazed by how few married women *are* solely housewives.)

Judgments made on the basis of stereotyped images are errors of logic. The reasoning goes like this: If most home-makers are women, then all women are homemakers. Very few men are ever asked if they are homemakers. Men at home are considered unemployed. We may never know if in-deed there is a silent minority of male homemakers.

Other stereotypes are just as misleading. Many women as-sume that successful businesswomen are naturally liberated. Some of the most unliberated women I have met are corpor-ate administrators. Liberation is a state of mind, not an occu-pation. Don't be surprised when liberated Carrie Career uses her sex appeal as a tool and Hannah Homemaker uses the ultimate in time-management procedures.

Judging by widespread media images, if our impressions were not tempered by our own experience, we could easily believe that all women are either housewives, mothers, or sex objects.

In most magazines geared for a general audience, the predominant image of woman is that of a sexually attractive inferior. The worst offenders of female sensitivity are the men's magazines such as *Playboy*, *Oui*, and the like, which exist by distorting the image of the female. As a result, many women feel that to some men they are "ducks in hunting season." These skin magazines dehumanize and objectify women. Photographic portrayals are not particularly cute or sexy, but can instill a feeling of power or dominance in the male reader viewing a nude and exploitable subject. Some men enjoy the special superiority gained from this type of voyeurism.

Most of us are outraged when we see child pornography. We fear these images may generate ideas in the minds of the unstable, making our children potential victims. We recognize exploitation of the very young. Yet, we are *not* outraged when we see adult women in pornographic situations. Do we not fear how these images affect women? Or do we not care? The fact is, both men and women accept the sexual degradation of women. Social (normative) acceptance of female abasement as a sexual object is harmful to healthy male and female relationships. (Magazines such as *Playgirl*, catering to a female audience, may depict men as chunks of beef, but the male image to-date has not been greatly affected by this depiction, since other stereotypic images of men are more readily available: the executive, the adventurer, etc.)

Physical attributes of the female are a focus of attention for the average male. Depending on his generation, he has learned to look at breasts, ass, or legs. This orientation is culturally supported by images seen daily. Generally, women do not regard penis size as a subject worthy of comment. But if men were commonly seen decorating the hoods of automobiles wearing tight, half-unzippered pants and serving drinks wearing aprons with a peek-a-boo hole near the groin, women would definitely take note of the male anatomy. If the media also supported this view of men, male crotches would become a focus of attention and we'd all start making comparisons.

Women will have attained a mark of social progress when magazines depicting women as sex objects are given the status of "watermelon jokes," which are no longer socially acceptable because of their insensitivity to black people.

Generalizing from a stereotype to an individual is how sexism manifests itself. Because we belong to a society in which female stereotypes are negative and possibly destructive, these generalizations can be damaging to female career aspirations and life plans.

Sexism is so strongly ingrained in our culture that one may not even recognize it when it appears. Have you ever felt uneasy or a little angered by something that was said, without knowing why?

Here's a simple test to determine if what took place was sexist. Substitute the words "black person" whenever you hear or read a statement directed toward a woman. If the statement sounds racist with the words "black person," then it is sexist with the word "woman." For example, I received a flyer one day describing the agenda of a business meeting. Another version of the agenda was also enclosed, with this statement printed across the top: "Please give this to your wife." Then I noticed that the other version of the agenda was simplified, implying "for your dumb wife!" I did the substitution test.

"Please give this to the black people." That statement was clearly racist! I almost missed the affront, but there was sexism staring me in the face.

LIVING THE ROLE

Others' expectations play a significant role in our view of ourselves. Women learn that they are supposed to be more beautiful, more peaceable, and more gracious than men. But women also learn that they are supposed to be weaker than men, not competitive or cut out for the world of business. Since our culture clearly values competitive attributes, being male is superior to being female. Consequently, women often *feel* inferior. Is it any wonder?

Men and women have both learned that it is appropriate for women to hold a one-down position. Women are taught to please men mainly for economic support. Women learn how to cater to others' needs. The nurturing by woman and the dominating by man appear as natural behaviors associated with each gender, but these behaviors are socially reinforced doctrines.

I remember learning how to dance when I was in junior high school. My natural tendency was to lead my male partner. I was told repeatedly, "You must let him lead. Anne, you're trying to be the leader. You must not do that." Although I was fundamentally aggressive, I had to learn to modify my actions. With effort and practice, I learned how to "follow" while dancing, but it was conscious and forced— hardly an instinctive reaction for me. (Later, I also learned how to mold my preferences and interests to suit my male partners.)

Most women will recall being taught to sit "with knees together," even if they wore slacks. The natural tendency is to relax one's legs, as boys and men do. Sitting ladylike requires unnatural effort and subtly lets a little girl know she can't do what boys can do. She gets the message: Certain behaviors are expected from her and she is not as free as her male counterpart.

As a result of the socialization process, many women trained to fit the married childbearer role are psychologically set up for a secondary position in their relationships with men. Self-degradation is not uncommon among women. In pursuit of male approval, women will do almost anything to please.

A woman might spend hours making cute picture birthday cards and baking brownies for a man on his birthday when he has never given her a birthday card. She will give him sexual pleasure but ask for none in return. She will knit a sweater to show her love. If a man were to do the same thing for such a woman, he would quickly lose her admiration. A woman with a low self-image cannot accept devotion from a man. He does not confirm her low evaluation of herself. If she believes she is worthless, he is obviously a fool if he loves her. Men who are "bastards" tend to be popular with women who place a low value on themselves. However, it is easy to understand why many women have damaged feelings of self-worth—our society perpetuates this image.

Men with a high self-image can easily accept all tributes. Men don't usually object to women who try to please and often marry the female devotee. Almost all men feel superior to women.

Unless our society changes, women who subjugate themselves will find marriage more easily attainable than women who demand equal time. Playing up to a male ego and fanning it when necessary will please most men. So much so, that he will marry the female devotee and keep her as long as she continues to flatter him, unless he tires of the act or meets someone who does it better.

Women refusing to play this game often marry later in life than is usual or not at all. Sometimes they will meet a man familiar with the old game or a man who prefers a more honest relationship. I do not want to imply that women who play the doormat game are dishonest—they simply have low self-images, often in spite of their actual accomplishments. (I know a professional woman, far more talented than her husband and who should have a high self-image, who willingly subjugated her promising career to his failing enterprises. He feels no pangs of conscience in accepting her subjugation. This phenomenon, although accepted as normal, is harmful to happiness.)

BODY MAKEUP:

Our bodies and the images we project say something about us. The way we look is also defined by cultural assumptions about our sex. Men shave their faces. Women shave their underarms and legs. Women will wear makeup; men will wear skin-bracer (though, of course, not all men or women follow these guidelines; many men sport beards and many women wear no makeup). The grooming rituals associated with gender help one to attain a more masculine or feminine image.

Male and female images are culturally defined. Yet the ancient Greek male shaved his body hair for aesthetic reasons. And as recently as 1950, European females posed in fashion magazines with the underarm au naturel.

You can determine the significance of "feminine grooming" in your own life by following the suggested body-image experiments. For a minimum of one month, allow the hair under your arms and on your legs to grow. Note your reactions during this period. See if you start to feel more powerful or more masculine. In this culture, because we associate hair in these parts of the anatomy with men, women may start to feel an uncanny sense of masculine power—much like the sense of power Samson had before his hair was shorn. (You may also notice that the underarms stay drier with a cushion of hair than without it.) You will also experience some disadvantages. Clothes options for the office may become limited in the same way as they do for men. (Men may want to shave their underarms and legs to experience a journey to the feminine.)

If the above experiment is too drastic, try this simpler one. If you wear makeup, go without it for a week. If you don't wear makeup, use it for a week. How do you feel? How has your perception of yourself changed? Do others notice or react? Women who wear makeup are often surprised by how dependent they are on cosmetics. They may feel "naked" and ugly without it when, in fact, few people notice the difference. Women who don't usually wear makeup should apply cosmetics and observe if their personalities change to match the image.

These experiments with image challenge your relationship to the definition of gender. You will know how strongly you feel about your own femininity or masculinity and how integral the image is to your identity. Our behaviors and images are learned and specific. For men to understand women and for women to understand men, we must, on occasion, exchange cultural clothing.

A Visit to a New Set

I arranged a visit to the Land of Perfect Marriage. It is a small town located in a small canyon. The mayor of the town greeted me at the airport upon my arrival. She explained that very few people bothered to visit the town. No one is interested in it except the occasional sociologist who comes to see the people who have happy marriages. I blushed. I admitted that even though I wasn't a sociologist that was my reason for visiting. I said, "Would you mind telling me about these marriages?" She said, "Well, it's very simple. Everyone here values his or her freedom and individuality quite highly, so we don't expect others to conform to our images. We accept people as they are. We have no family unit. We are all individuals."

I was confused. "What do you mean?"

She smiled. "Each person is recognized as unique. Family unit membership is secondary. Everyone uses his or her given name, each person is free to work, to keep his or her own money, and to buy and sell property. You see," she added, "marriage and the rules that go with it are decided by the couple."

"But is that marriage?" I asked.

"Marriage is what you want it to be. Our people want it to be happy and to provide each other with the space to be themselves. Yet they also acknowledge their desire to continue their relationship."

"Well, what about children?"

"Couples here agree on whether or not to have children. Each child is guided by responsible parents, but that child is also entitled to individual rights. Children and parents make contracts with each other."

"What happens if one partner meets a more attractive mate?"

She laughed. "Adultery. There is no need for it."

"But surely it must occur," I responded.

"Everyone here realizes there is more than one suitable lifetime companion. If one person meets a more suitable mate, they discuss the situation. It can be part of the original agreement. Since no one owns anyone, the marriage agreement is either broken or changed to meet the new situation. Because there are few surprises, we rarely see unhappiness over that sort of thing. Usually it occurs when couples pair too young. But most people are happy in their marriages."

"Are there rules about the age one can marry?" I asked.

"No. However, since marriage is an agreement, or contract, defined by the couple, most do not leap into marriage and usually, after the contract is drawn, the younger ones change their minds. Most contracts are renewed yearly on the marriage date. Since there is no pressure here to get married, people tend to marry later than the average age for the country. Couples desiring children wait until they are financially comfortable. Having children is an individual decision—there is no social pressure."

I thanked the mayor for her time and toured the main street. The people I saw walked with a spirited gait. Glowing, smiling faces reflected their happy hearts.

Reviewing the Program

As marrieds, it is easy to fall into a life patterned after traditional social expectations. The wife administers all correspondence and social engagements. She is asked by everyone she meets, "What does your husband do?" Her status depends upon his occupation. His success is important because, since they are one in the traditional marital arrangement, his success is their success. It is assumed that in the marriage there is a mutual respect for one another and a desire to work together in the interest of family life.

The roles of husband and wife are ready-made. In most marriages, traditionally based, there is a sharp division of labor. Even if the woman works outside the home, she still is "the keeper of the house." The so-called liberated married woman in the work force appears to have traded one job for two. The man with a working wife is still considered the head of the household, or main breadwinner, regardless of the size of his paycheck.

The full-time homemaker works long hours and is financially dependent on her husband. He supports her so that she can maintain the home and care for children. The family structure is taken for granted. We don't think about it, we just do it—but is it the best way?

I have witnessed happy people in traditionally structured marriages. I have also witnessed mutually dependent and miserable people in this type of marital arrangement. People are not always, but often, trapped by the Blessed Assumptions of marriage. If you like traps, it's great. Personally, I enjoy freedom, and it is clear to both my husband and myself that we remain married out of free choice. Our only dependency is emotional—our love and affection for one another.

A good relationship can become limited by the roles assumed in marriage, and one's happiness may be limited by conforming to social expectations. While some couples are happy with the old program, does the traditional structure work for you? Or do you feel trapped?

There are countless books on the subject of marriage, but the truth is that there is *no* answer applicable to everyone. You are the expert on your marriage. You are the only one who can identify what *you* want out of your life. Your parents, friends, and others have told you what *they* expect from you. If what you want differs from what others expect, you may experience unhappiness and conflict.

What other people expect is irrelevant.

What matters is what you want.

What you want is what will make you happy (unless you are a masochist).

What's wrong is that *others'* expectations may not contribute to *your* self-fulfillment.

CHAPTER **5**

Sex for Sale

"And that's about as fur as she could go. . . ."

WOMEN REALIZE THAT THEIR PHYSICAL ATTRACTIVENESS and nurturing qualities are good selling points for future mates. A few centuries ago a woman's body could literally be bought. Her purchase price was based on her looks, the services she could provide (sex was only one of them), and her ability to produce offspring (a source of labor). Both slaves and purchased women had two things in common—total economic dependency and no real power.

The Marriage Market

If a woman's economic survival is dependent upon a man, then in order to prosper she must become valuable to him. In our culture, women are trained from birth to become "pretty things" in response to a male ideal. If a woman has no real earning capability, what other choice does she have?

Women make themselves attractive to men in a variety of ways in order to increase their desirability and their price. Developing assets that please men guarantees survival for women in a society where women are assumed to be economically dependent.

Men also try to make themselves desirable to women. They generally accomplish this objective by increasing their dollar-earning ability. A man's appearance and charm are often secondary to his occupation in importance. A woman's occupation, though, is generally secondary to her looks. Before meeting a woman for the first time, a man might ask, "Is she good-looking?" A woman asks about a man, "What does he do?"

The male in our society still has greater earning potential than the female. He feels little social pressure to glorify his sex appeal in order to get a job or to attract a woman. He develops his physical appeal mainly to gain points in the bedroom. He does not need handsome looks as a drawing card for financial support. If he has a large bank account, he is—handsome or not—surprisingly attractive to most women.

I am reminded of the old saying handed down from mother to daughter: "It's as easy to love a rich man as a poor one." A woman is expected to gain status through marriage, and generally "sells" herself for "better" and not for "worse." Men sell themselves as providers. Both are caught in a trap that is equally oppressive.

Attracting the right man is important to a woman because if she doesn't find someone she loves, she may be forced to marry someone she doesn't love—for dollar support alone. Because these economic relationships are so important to woman's survival, what she has to sell is crucial. Like a fisherman, the woman casts out a lure. The man wants to snap up the bait and is happy to be known as a "good catch."

Women misuse their power when they sell sex. Men misuse their power by flaunting dollar bills—the better with which to attract you, my dear. Love, the chameleon, appears to adapt to the man with money and the woman with mammae.

SEX, THE DECLINING COMMODITY

When we think of the sale of sex, we think of the person who sells sex as a commodity—the prostitute. Dollar bills are exchanged for intercourse. Why does prostitution exist? What bearing does it have on male and female relationships?

We all sell something. It could be a specific service sold to our employer or a bubbling personality sold to the public-relations department. Our society says it is okay to sell these things for dollars. However, it is illegal to sell sex for dollars. Nevertheless, sex can be sold for marriage.

How, then, does the prostitute differ from the "virtuous" woman? Both are social creations. Both sell sex. The street-walker sells sex for money but will not sell love or emotional ties. For the male or female customer this proposition can be attractive. The payee experiences dominance and power over another person. Men and women who purchase sex may be "getting back" at someone else or using this means to express hostility toward the opposite sex. Or perhaps they simply cannot get what they want any other way.

Traditionally, women have been told to stay "virtuous" for marriage; once married, she has lost much of her bargaining power. Therefore, the woman who keeps her "virtue," not for her own good reasons, but as a bargaining point for marriage, is selling sex. The man who wants her, buys her through marriage; once married, she has lost much of her bargaining power and he can gain control over her.

The degree to which sex will decline as a commodity will be the degree to which women gain equal access to the marketplace and become financially independent. Women will no longer need to sell their bodies, personalities, or capacity to nurture. Women and men will some day play the same economic game by the same rules under the same set of circumstances. With the future decline of sex as a commodity, women and men will find themselves better able to explore honest and rewarding relationships. Women will not sell sex. And men won't buy it.

A BODY IN TRADE

When women were chattel for trade and in almost the same position as slaves, the commodity was the whole person. Today, at least in this country, slaves are no longer bought; women are no longer chattel. But, as mentioned previously, vestiges of this kind of slavery still exist, and as long as women do not have full access to dollar earning power, men will have the capacity to dominate them. Money *is* power. Unequal economic opportunity between the sexes has forced many women to sell their bodies for marriage or, literally, to sell their bodies on the street. This is not to say that selling sex cannot be profitable. Some of the richest women in the world have made their fortunes through these sales. The fact that a woman sells sex to gain riches, whereas a man need not, is a social inequity unfair to both and degrading to women.

There are all kinds of buying going on between the sexes and we'd be fools to say that it doesn't happen. It may happen to you while you are almost unaware of it. Sex between buyers happens every time someone owes sexual "role playing" to another person for some other reason than friendship.

If the guy pays for your rent, your baby-sitter, or your contraceptives, he figures you owe him—sex, or cooking, or doing his laundry. That's sex between buyers. If he gives you gifts and you figure you owe him, that's sex between buyers.*

* *So You Don't Want to Be a Sex Object* (Denver, Colo.: RMP Publications, 1970).

Women are taught to accept the role of submission. Men are taught to accept the role of domination. Several social institutions—including marriage—keep women in their place. Men, fearful of losing their superior position, and women, fearful of losing their dependent status, fight against women's political, economic, and social equality by citing the "horrible" effect this would have on family life. The "horrible" effect of women's equality would be the loss of male domination.

A New Deal

Living up to the expectations of others, adhering to roles based on sex, and falling into stereotypes are easy. Creating a marriage that will allow you both to live the free, honest lives you want to lead is *hard work*.

For me, marriage could have been the end of my professional career had I succumbed to social pressure. Instead, I fought to retain my professional position. I also argued with my husband about keeping my name, separating my money, getting my own space, and sharing housework. As two strong individualists who value independence, freedom, and each other, we were able to find solutions to our problems; but first we had to discard preconceived notions and assumptions about marriage.

Think for yourself. Cast off the old notions. Don't sell out. Release yourself from the Blessed Assumptions, the social roles, and the sex stereotypes that plague married life.

The next part of this book explains how a marriage of seemingly irreconcilable differences was made to work, how a property system and marriage structure developed, and how these principles could be applied by you to your marriage.

Part III

Regaining Your Identity, Independence, and Freedom

CHAPTER **6**

Your Name—Your Identity

"I know I musn't fall into the pit, but when I'm with a feller—I fergit! . . ."

CORRECTING WHAT'S WRONG IN YOUR MARRIAGE means shifting the structural base. An excellent place to begin, once you decide to do this, is on the label of your marriage package. Giving up your own name on the altar of marriage undercuts your individuality. When you become "Mrs. John Jones" you say to the world, "I am John Jones' wife. This is my role; this is my station." For many women, losing their name creates an identity crisis. Your name *is* your identity. Many women have suffered "name loss" in silence, enduring, then finally accepting, their "wife of" status.

Post-Ceremony Crisis

During the first year of marriage, I found myself tormented by this identity crisis and learned the truth of the oft-stated pronouncement that "the first year of marriage is the hardest." Territories and consequent power relationships are established during this first year as are a variety of games for newlyweds to play. Right off the bat, it seemed, we were in trouble: I wanted to keep my name.

Having been attached to my label of twenty-six years, I could not understand why I had to change it. None of the arguments—"It's a social convention," "It's the law," and "Why? Don't you love your husband?"—seemed good enough to me. Part of my attachment to my name could be attributed to the fact that I really liked myself—it had taken me years to reach that psychological point. In a world of rapid changes, the one stable element providing continuity was my name. My husband argued, "Shouldn't we both have the same last name? You'll embarrass me. How can I introduce you to my friends?"

I argued, "Then why don't you take my name?" Of course, that was intolerable.

An identity crisis is disorienting. One feels lost, misplaced, and upset. Not everyone experiences this crisis, but a lost identity is not the only reason to keep your own name. You may want to retain your name because it describes you as independent, because it will be easier for friends to locate you, because it will simplify financial transactions, or because you like the way it sounds.

If you do take back your given name, you will be surprised at the results of this action. It will rattle the shackles of your marriage and the neighbors on the block. But you will not be the first or last woman to shake the world this way. In England, in 1797, Mary Wollstonecraft (author of *Vindication of the Rights of Woman*) and William Godwin created a scandal by retaining their own names and careers after marriage. Later, in 1855, Lucy Stone, the famous woman's suffrage advocate, and Henry Blackwell did the same. History books seldom mention these precedents. Stone and Blackwell wrote in their marriage contract:

While we acknowledge our mutual affection by publicly assuming the relationship of husband and wife, we deem it a duty to declare that this act on our part implies no sanction of, nor promise of, voluntary obedience to such of the present laws of marriage that refuse to recognize the wife as an independent rational being, while they confer upon the husband an injurious and natural superiority.*

The custom of women adopting their husbands' names originated with English common law, according to which wives are legal nonentities. Adoption of a man's name aptly described his wife's relationship to him in the marriage—the subservient one. She was proud to bear his name because it gave her the only status she had in a male-dominated society and was a label that reflected her status in the marital structure. She could be conveniently identified as either an important or unimportant personage through her husband's label.

You and I know you are much more than a wife. But if you are sure you are comfortable with your label, there is no need to change it or to read further into this chapter.

A ROSE IS A ROSE

How important is a name to you? By any other name you may smell just as sweet—this is true for roses, anyway.

But people, unlike roses, are identified by names. Each person is different and does not smell equally as sweet as everyone else. That is why we differentiate by name. People call you by that name and you respond. You write it where it says "Name." It is yours.

* Susan Edmiston, "How to Write Your Own Marriage Contract," *Ms.*, Spring 1972, p. 68.

A name is a means of identification; it is a shorthand designation of everything that serves to make an individual identifiable and unique: appearance, background, personality, intelligence, and ideals. An individual realizes early in life this essential connection between a particular sound and the individual's self-image.

It is not sufficient, however, to state that whatever meaning a name possesses is derived from the self it symbolizes; in addition, the definition and development of that self may partially depend on the name it bears. A surname may establish a particular ethnic identity or family background, a source of kinship with other individuals in which one may take considerable pride. Thus, on the one hand, a name may impose the perspective of a particular tradition on one's view of oneself; on the other hand, as identification it is a symbolic representation of an entire individual. Its importance is increased by its constant use; the equation of symbol = self is reinforced every time one signs a check or answers a call. Seen in such a context, it is clear that changing the name of an adult woman is not a trivial matter. For twenty or thirty years she has used her maiden name to identify herself; it reflects her link with her family and symbolizes a process of development spanning her lifetime. Now she is to define herself in new terms, terms that emphasize that now she is a dependent, a wife before she is an individual. Her name does not now reflect her background, but that of her husband; it does not embody her development and achievements, but his.

Thus, a change of surname is but one more factor in our society that tends to inhibit independent development.*

Established by custom and, taken at face value, a nice romantic notion, adoption of your husband's name is potentially destructive to your happiness because it robs you of your individual status. To a man, assumption of his name by a woman is a symbol of his broadening influence in life. To a woman, the surrender of her name and adoption of her hus-

* Margaret Eve Spencer, "A Woman's Right to Her Name," *UCLA Law Review*, vol. 21, no. 2 (December 1973), pp. 665–690.

band's surname represents the beginning of a new life under his protectorship. Your husband's label remains the same. Your label says you are married and to whom—two private pieces of information, unrelated to who *you* are, that identify you in terms of your relationship to someone else. Your status depends on him. And that dependent status can affect your happiness.

STRADDLING THE FENCE

Faced with the postceremony identity crisis, I argued with my husband and myself. He wanted me to take his name. I wanted my own name. Every time I received mail addressed to "Mr. and Mrs." I felt depressed. When, by some error, I received mail addressed in my own name, I was secretly happy. My husband didn't understand. Since I was a professional woman I used "the professional-woman argument." Because I had published (twice!) and everyone knew me by my former name, I said I should keep my own name "for professional reasons." That argument sounded reasonable. But it was schizophrenic—I had one name professionally and one name socially. In today's world, where social and professional communities mix, my identity problem was confounded. Who was I? Finally, I thought I had the solution. I would hyphenate my name, keeping my own name first—for professional reasons, of course. (This practice is common in England to show lineage.) Reluctantly, my husband allowed me this license, but he would not hyphenate *his* name. Merrily hyphenated, I changed all my records and informed my friends. But hyphenation was awkward. Half the computers dropped the hyphen, giving me my husband's name; friends would forget one of the names or reverse the order. Now I had three names: a hyphenated name, my given name, and his name.

My husband suffered my wrath, but didn't alter his position. I was miserable. Distressed for months over this dilemma, I finally exploded when my student ID number, which I had had for years, was changed because the computer could not adjust to a hyphen. In a fit of assertive energy, no longer compromising, I announced one day to my husband and to the world that I would take back my own name. My husband was exasperated. He thought I would change my mind. But that day marked the beginning of a new relationship with my husband. My heart lifted with joy. I felt free. And a year later, he asked me, "Why don't women use their own names?"

Staking the Claim to Your Own Name

In staking the claim to your own name, you are not rejecting your husband. You are simply not rejecting yourself. Ask him to use your given name instead of his name for one day. When he can't accept your proposal, you can thank him for understanding.

At times you will actually wonder whether you're doing the right thing because few people will agree or support your efforts. Your parents, his parents, and those closest to you may voice loud objections. Do not try to gain their approval or agreement on something they may never understand. Be prepared for the question, "Don't you love your husband?"

Be more tolerant of your family than you might be toward others. My parents, who I thought would be pleased, were shocked when I kept my name. Eight years later, they finally addressed mail to their daughter in her own name.

It may be that you have been married for so long that returning to your former name would now be an identity crisis. You are the best judge of what is right for you. Try this simple role-reversal exercise and see for yourself:

Pretend you are at a party, an important social event. Many old acquaintances are there. You meet a former classmate.

Introduce your husband by his first name and your given surname. "Hi, Alice, I'd like you to meet —— ——."

1. How did you feel?
2. Did your perception of your husband change?
3. Was he an extension of yourself? Was he his own person?

Try it again. This time introduce him as Mr. (*your given
name*).
Repeat questions 1, 2, and 3.

A woman who wants her own name *should* take it back.
No other reason is needed. You'll be surprised at what difference a seemingly little thing like a name can make toward
restructuring a relationship. Suddenly you are autonomous
again. Stand up for yourself. No one else will.

A married woman who wants to regain her own name will
have fun and excitement playing the Name-Change Game.
Some amusing experiences await you, since most people will
attempt to give you your husband's name anyway. Be persistent. Stay calm. But get what you want. Despite many
precedents, you are a pioneer, and pioneers have never had it
easy. You are also paving the way for a new and better marital relationship, and, although now he's not sure, your husband
will love you more when he sees an independent and happier you.

Remember—the name you use consistently (not for fraudulent purposes) is legally your name. You do not need a lawyer
to change it. An individual may change her name under the
principle of common law merely by adopting and using a
different name. Do not allow anyone to convince you that you
must use your husband's name or that this action represents
something basically wrong with you, your marriage, or your
psyche. Whatever you do, use only one name. Do not use
both the professional name and a married name. If you do,
the purpose of establishing your own identity in order to at-

tain a healthy equal relationship with your husband will be defeated.

People will need time to readjust to your name change. Your husband can support you by introducing you properly to his friends and associates. Let us say, for example, that you are Janet Davies married to a man named Richard Burke. He should introduce you by saying, "I'd like you to meet my wife, Janet Davies." If he has difficulty, introduce yourself: "Hello, I'm Janet Davies." That you are married is no one's business. However, if people insist on querying about your marital status, you can explain, "I prefer to use my own name." Or, "We are married, but we each prefer to use our own name."

Hosts and hostesses become bumbling idiots when introducing a married couple with different names. They giggle like teenagers or add their own explanation—"But they are married." People resist the unconventional, but eventually learn. Help your friends and hosts. Tell them how they may introduce you: "This is Janet Davies." "This is Richard Burke." Astonishingly simple.

Announce to everyone you know that you are now using your own name instead of your husband's. Do not refer to your given name as a "maiden name," since you are not regressing to a previous life. You are using *your own name*, because marriage is a continuation of your life and you are your own person. Your "legal name" is the name you use.

You will need to change all records that bear your old name: credit cards, stock and bond records, driver's license and automobile title, Social Security, income tax and employment records, telephone listings, property deeds, insurance policies, voter's registration, passport, and club memberships. Get new credit cards, new driver's license, and Social Security card (your number remains the same). But do not try to change everything at once. Request the name change when cards expire or licenses must be renewed. The reason? Say, "marriage" and save yourself time explaining. Here are a few tips from the Name Choice Center for California Women: *

Credit Cards:

Insist on your right to credit in your own name. Department stores have become more adaptable to this practice over the years, but be prepared for those stores with outdated policies, such as "only one card to a family" and "only the husband's name on a card." One way to avoid this hassle is simply to apply for credit as "Ms." Write "not applicable" in the space provided for "husband's name."

Driver's License:

To get back your own name, complete a "change of name" form—the same one you may have used when you married. Again, state the reason for changing your name as "Marriage."

Income Tax and Employment Records:

Married couples can file separate or joint income tax returns using different names. However, IRS clerks may be confused. Explain in writing on the top of the form that you have not made an error—you choose to use your own name.

If you are newly employed, be sure that your first paycheck is in your name. Clerks (thinking they've caught an error) will assign your husband's surname on your check if they know his name.

Telephone and Other Listings:

Get your *own* listing. It symbolizes your existence on this planet and will enable people to reach you. Call your local phone company and ask for the additional listing. The monthly cost, if any, will be small. Also, plant your name alongside your husband's on the mailbox.

---

* Pat Montandon, a pioneer for name choice, is founder of the Name Choice Center for California Women (P.O. Box 3532, San Francisco, CA 94119). Write to her for the coordinator in your area if you encounter any problems.

Passports:

A married woman can use her own name on a passport, although if she has not used her own name throughout the marriage, she must submit evidence that she has used her own name publicly and exclusively for a substantial period of time. If you encounter obstacles, ask for the supervisor.

Insurance:

Change insurance companies if the agent refuses to use your name and not that of your husband.

Voting:

Legally, you can use your own name. If the clerk doesn't believe this is so, contact your local election board or state representative.

General Policy:

There's no need for anyone to know your husband's name. You will be amazed by how unnecessary his name becomes once you don't mention it. I never volunteer my husband's name—I therefore eliminate *all risk* of getting it. I reveal his full name only when asked or when I introduce him to others.

And never apologize to anyone for using your own name! Keep explanations to one sentence.

To speed the transition, order stationery with your name (or both names). Use your old personalized stationery for scrap paper or write your own name over the other one.

But What About the Children?

Traditionally, children are given the father's surname. Legally, you are free to name your child whatever pleases you, including Sun Beam even if your last name isn't Beam. Children are more accepting and adaptable than adults. To establish a maternal line, mothers may want to give their surname to their daughters. Your preference, however, can be foiled by hospital personnel. Know the chapter and section of the law before you enter the hospital and do not sign the final birth certificate form until it is satisfactory. Hospital personnel may take the liberty to complete or "correct" the form if you don't demand the last word.

A Pre-Nuptial Note

If you are now planning to marry and you don't want to assume your husband's surname, print a note on your wedding announcement stating, "The bride will retain her own name after marriage." Though this message will shock some people, it will save you problems later. (Deciding after marriage that you want your name back is a more difficult ordeal than deciding later that you would like his name after all.) When people call you by your husband's name anyway, politely correct them. When you enclose your new address card with your wedding announcement, be sure to use both names. If your friends complain about the inconvenience of writing two full names, you might suggest an abbreviation: M/M Davies/ Burke

For example:

AT HOME

Ms. Janet Davies

Mr. Richard Burke

1531 Milvia Street
Franklin Springs, Ohio

Starting your marriage using your own name, or regaining your name after years of marriage, requires vigilance and patience. It may take a year before people start calling you by your given name. The label on your marriage package symbolizes your relationship and describes the structure. It states what is inside: two people, two names.

CHAPTER **7**

Money Matters

"My uncle out in Texas . . . he signs his checks with X's, but they cash them just the same."

BAD RELATIONSHIPS CAN BE IMPROVED and good partnerships maintained through proper money allocation. Money problems arising in marriage generally stem from a practical and accepted financial arrangement—shared income. This arrangement, however, is devastating to personal freedom and reduces the potential for a happy marriage.

When people marry, both lose independence. The husband traditionally becomes responsible for support, and the wife—even if she has her own income—dependent. Ideally, expenditures large and small are decided together. Yet when one partner spends from the general pool without the concurrence of the other, you can bet an argument results. When buried resentments do surface, the outburst is a virulent explosion

73

of displaced anger. Lovers appear trapped in this way, in a mutually dependent and guilt-laden affair. For instance, John wants to buy a jacket and Sally wants to buy an exotic Japanese vase. John says he makes more money than Sally and argues that he therefore has the right to spend that money for what he wants. Sally counters with the assertion that the world doesn't allow her to earn as much money as John. But, in fact, John earns more money. Consequently, John always buys what he wants. Sally becomes resentful because she cannot buy the vase and John feels guilty after he buys his new jacket. The next morning they argue about the toast.

Over the course of seven years, my husband and I have developed a way of handling money which works, sparing us almost all arguments over money. The system, based on separate incomes, is called the Separate Property System. When two people have incomes, there is no need to share both incomes, even if each is very different in dollars. (Homemakers must learn how to negotiate for what their work is worth, as discussed in detail in Chapter 8.)

This Separate Property System was created when I had *no* income other than a small stipend from my fellowship, and my husband held a lucrative corporate position. In the pages ahead, you can learn how it worked for us and how you too can use it. But if you and your partner share the same visions, agree on *everything*, and *never* argue over money, skip to the next chapter.

Our Separate Property System

Like almost everyone else, we started our marriage with little money, and following what appeared to be a reasonable pattern, pooled our resources into one nest egg. With few common values and interests, every potential purchase resulted in an argument. We discussed endlessly how that money should be spent. I wanted to make long-distance phone calls. He said it was a waste of money. I had always used the phone freely and was annoyed by his criticism. He bought a motorcycle. I said if he bought a motorcycle, then I should be able to make long-distance phone calls. After all, it was *our* money.

When we were single, we never argued over money. We never needed permission to purchase anything we wanted. Why did we need it now? Because when we had married, we'd agreed with the Blessed Assumptions.

The solution to our money problems was simple. We separated our money, reasoning that if each controlled his/her own money we would not argue over it. I had $300 a month income from my fellowship. Our apartment rent was $200 a month. I paid half the rent, which meant I was left with $200 a month to spend on books, supplies, half the food bill, and, best of all, those long-distance phone calls. I was able to support myself again.

He had more disposable income than I and bought a range of items I would never have agreed to purchase. But he purchased what *he* wanted, whether or not I approved, with no infringement on my purchasing power. We were both happy.

With this economic arrangement, I found the way to freedom and dignity within marriage. Money relationships were clearly defined; no one person was dependent or trapped or pressured to earn.

You may think the Separate Property System is impossible to implement, especially after years of marriage. Separating your property is *not* easy (ask any divorced person) and maintaining the system is work. When each partner has control and management of his or her own property in marriage, an enormous burden is lifted from both, and the wife's identity does not depend on how much money the *husband* makes. People using the Separate Property System do not live through one another. They are free to make their own future financial plans. And, in the event of a failing marriage, couples will not stay together because of financial considerations alone. Being married does not make husband and wife one person. A person with money power, even if poor, is a free person.

Untying the Money Knots

Among married couples, money is usually deposited in and withdrawn from joint accounts, such as savings and checking accounts. In order to operate as a financial independent in marriage, separate accounts are necessary. If you have placed your money together in a joint account, you must separate it again.

Since marital property laws are regulated by the individual states, you should know the laws in *your* state concerning property for married couples in case you decide to divorce. Changes are occurring that may affect you, and it is important to keep abreast. For example, the law has changed in California since I married in 1969. California is a community-property law state. That means that (with certain exceptions) property acquired after marriage, including your own income, is community property. However, everything you owned *before* you married, including your own income and gifts, (unless commingled) remains separate property. Although the community-property law was developed to protect women, it was based on the Blessed Assumption that husband and wife are one, and that one is the providing husband. Major inequities resulted. Although the respective interests of husband and wife in the community property were supposedly protected, the property was under the management and control of the husband. (I'll never forget the day I tried to open an account with a brokerage firm and was told to get written "permission" from my husband. As a single woman, of course, I could have opened an account easily.)

Under California's community-property law, the wife automatically inherited her husband's debts to the extent of her share of the community property, whereas the husband was only responsible for providing basic necessities to the household and for his wife's debts providing he signed an agreement with her creditors. The husband also had the right to his wife's paycheck and could collect it from her employer. You can imagine the abuses that occurred.

On October 10, 1972 I testified before the California Senate Judiciary Committee with many other women unfairly affected by these community-property statutes to challenge the law. As a result, effective January 1, 1975, each spouse—husband *and* wife—has management and control of the community property. This means married women can open and close charge accounts and buy and sell stock shares without their husbands' consent. Also, they can now have their own charge accounts without their husbands' signature and establish credit on the basis of their own earnings. Both spouses are liable for each other's debts and, upon dissolution of the marriage, the community property is divided equally.

Community property is a distinct entity. Simply, with certain exceptions, it is the real property in a community-property state and assets acquired during the marriage. Separate property is all assets acquired prior to marriage which have not been commingled with community property.

However, under community-property law, you *can* establish your own separate property after marriage by a written agreement with your spouse (see Chapter 14). But it must, in fact, be maintained separately and not commingled with other community property. Today eight states are governed by community-property laws (Arizona, California, Idaho, Louisiana, Nevada, New Mexico, Texas, and Washington). In the remaining states, laws vary, but generally women who are married (unless they keep their assets in their name alone) do not own or cannot exercise control over jointly held property.

Based on my own experience, I believe married couples can

and should maintain their own accounts, regardless of state of residence, for a happier state of mind. Two contented people make a better marriage. And if dissolution of the marriage should occur, the wife would be protected—her credit, finances, and psyche will all remain intact.

HOW TO SEPARATE MONEY

Joint savings, checking, and charge accounts can be closed, and separate accounts opened. If you have been married for a long time, you may have difficulty recalling your contribution to joint accounts. You may decide to halve everything or to negotiate a settlement based on an estimate of contributed funds (or services, if you are a homemaker).

When you try to regain control of your own charge account with stores, you will quickly realize what rights you lost as a result of marriage. It is work. First, close your existing joint account and inform the store that you want your own account. Generally, you will be accommodated. However, if the store has a reactionary policy, re-apply, but be sure to provide no information about your husband on the application. Use your own name (not your husband's name). Do not lie about your legal marital status, since that is fraudulent; simply do not answer any questions about your husband. Insert the initials "N.A.," for "not applicable," in any spaces provided for information about your husband. If you are questioned, state that your account is to be given on the basis of *your* own financial merits, since you will be the only one using the card and the only one paying the bills.

Similar advice applies to men. Do not give any information about your wife, or else you will find that she may use your card and you will be responsible for the bills. Or the store may decide to give you a joint account—exactly what you don't want. Married men may, by the way, run into clerks who suspect them of having a mistress for whom they wish to purchase items. So if you get some strange looks, that's probably the reason.

Men still have it easier than women when it comes to opening a separate account. However, theoretically and legally, there is no reason a married woman cannot have her own charge account. If you run into a problem, do *not* discuss it with the clerk. The clerk is paid to follow policy. Ask for the department head and tell him or her that the store's policy is discriminatory. Talk only to the people who can make decisions. Remember, you are fighting for your and your husband's mutual independence so that a love based on equal partnership is possible. Be persistent in your pursuit.

In charge of your own money, you can spend it as you wish. Items for yourself and the household will be purchased with cash, credit cards, and checks. In all cases, receipts are available, but a way to share and record the household expenses is needed. To use the Separate Property System, joint and personal purchases must first be identified and then tallied.

A joint purchase is a purchase that you both recognize as one you both desire to use or consume. An item that only you want is a personal purchase. Every day you will spend money —some for items only you want and some for joint purchases of items you both want and both will use, for which your partner is obligated to pay half.

After a little experience with the system, you will learn to recognize easily a joint purchase. As a rule of thumb, never purchase anything you think is "joint" without telling your partner first. For example, if you both read the newspaper, the newspaper is a joint purchase. If, however, you subscribe to *New Woman* magazine and he reads it, it is probably not joint because he would not subscribe to it himself.

You may wonder, "How am I going to keep track of all these joint purchases?" The answer is simple—just ask yourself, "How did I do it when I was single?" Chances are, you kept an account of expenses. You identified the joint ex-

penses, you tallied them, and you and your roommate set-
tled the account. Do the same with your husband.

TALLYING JOINT EXPENSES

Tallying the expenditures each month demands time and
energy, but is a small price to pay for financial independence.
The burden of bookkeeping can be eased by writing a "J"
after the check number or on your cash receipt to indicate
a joint expense. Review your checkbook monthly and list "J"
checks on a sheet of paper. Add to this list your collection of
"J" receipts for cash purchases.

In the case of my husband and me, at first we used a
wooden box on my office wall for depositing receipts. Every
time I used cash to make a purchase that was joint, I wrote a
"J" on the receipt and deposited it in the box. My husband
did the same. The problem with this method was that at the
end of the month the chits and receipts had to be sorted.
Keeping a file with our own chits and receipts proved easier.

Below is what a typical monthly tally of joint expenses might
look like (not your traditional love note).

From this tally, Jan owes Drew $10 ($35.22 minus $25.22).
Notice that also included here are expenses that were not
joint. For example, Drew asked Jan to buy him two pairs of
socks on her way home, so Drew owed Jan for the price of the
socks.

Seldom have my husband and I owed each other more than
$10 when all expenses were tallied. It is surprising how much,
in fact, both partners spend for joint purchases and how close
the tallies come each month. Regardless, even if there is no
monetary difference, there is a big difference on the happier
side for you both.

You will discover some things are best handled by one or
the other partner. For example, my husband is able to get
excellent insurance rates, so he takes care of the house in-

To Jan   From Drew

You owe me:
  Joint Expenses   And:
    7.30 groceries   20.00 cash loan
    2.00 window cleaner
    1.65 chicken   TOTAL
    6.59 gas
   12.90 dinner   35.22
   ─────
   ½(30.44)= 15.22

To: Drew   From: Jan

You owe me:
  Joint Expenses   And:
   $8.50 groceries $7.00 Socks
    .50 newspaper
  14.44 dinner
   5.00 pharmacy
   8.00 plant for house
  ─────
  ½(36.44)= $18.22   Total = $25.22

surance and charges me accordingly. These expenses are
tallied each month, receipts attached, and paid up. Now we
would never go back to a shared-money system.

As a general rule, schedule your tally meeting at a time
during the month when you pay the rent or discuss money

matters. Tally the expenses each month. (This chore takes about thirty minutes.) Another benefit is that you will both know exactly where your money is going.

NEGOTIATING JOINT EXPENSES:

What happens when you want something for the house that your husband doesn't want? Who pays for the couch? Let us assume that (1) we both want a couch for the living room, and (2) we want to spend no more than $300 for it. But I find a couch I love for $500. My husband says he is only willing to spend $150 for his half of the agreed $300. I must then decide if it is worth the extra $200 out of my own pocket to get the more expensive one. If so, my ownership of the couch has increased, yet he is not compromised. If the couch is sold, I will get back 70 percent of the sale, whereas he will get back 30 percent. If my husband doesn't want a couch and I do, I pay the entire price and own it 100 percent.

Another way to handle this type of situation is through a budget to which each partner contributes a specified sum each week or month to a particular expense category. When it is time to buy, money is drawn from that pocket. This approach is dangerous, however, because unless you both agree beforehand on how that money is to be spent, one partner may (with all good intent) draw money from the budget pocket without consulting the other partner. Budgets are also dangerous because they put your money together again. Nevertheless, for a specific purchase, some couples may find this method works best for them.

Yet another way of dividing expenses is for each partner to assume total responsibility for a certain expense category. For example, he pays all the water bills, she pays all the electric bills, and so on. By splitting expenses this way, the necessity of tallying and billing each other every month is avoided. However, the major drawback of the system is that an ex-

pense category may change, giving one partner an unequal
share of the financial burden.

Money can also be separated into—you guessed it—His, Hers,
and Ours checkbooks. This also is not a good idea, since the
"Ours" checkbook pools your money together again and unless you both agree on *everything*, your partner may un-
wittingly spend what you wanted to save.

By the way—no cheating is allowed, and you must trust
your partner. (If your money were shared, your partner could
easily spend it without telling you.) The Separate Property
System was not developed to promote unfair play. It was
developed so that both can operate with financial independence to enhance the joy of marriage.

But how can the Separate Property System work if one
partner is unemployed? To be unemployed means that you
were once employed or have the potential to be employed and
receive no pay for any labor. An unemployed mate is neither
providing services in the home nor outside the home for
which he/she is compensated in dollars. (See Chapter 8 for
arrangements to pay the homemaker.)

In this situation, the working spouse could provide a loan
to the unemployed spouse. The working partner is also free
not to loan any money (or may have no money to loan), in
which case the unemployed partner is in the same financial
position as any unmarried person. If possible, the bank,
friends, or relatives are called to the rescue.

My husband and I have an arrangement whereby we loan
dollars back and forth to each other when needed at a reasonable interest rate (usually one percent above the current
savings-and-loan passbook rate) and stipulate the date all
monies are due. We also use our loan agreement sometimes
for purchasing major items. For example, I wanted a car I
couldn't afford. My husband gave me a loan for the car and
I paid it back in six months.

We have agreed that if one partner loses income, and personal savings become exhausted, the other partner is obligated to provide a loan.

However, if one partner is unemployed, not looking for employment, or not providing any services, this partner's income (support) would be generated either by the working partner or through another source. In a relationship where the unemployed partner receives all of his/her income or support from the employed partner (not in recognition for any work or time contribution), the negotiating ability between them is severely diminished. I would hardly recommend they adopt the System.

But if this unemployed partner does nothing all day but eat bonbons in bed and receive monthly dividend checks in the mail, he/she then has the ability to use the Separate Property System with gusto.

You simply need your own money. The chips you use must be recognized as chips that belong to you—whether they are earned, loaned, or granted.

You might be thinking, "Well, what you've described so far is a lot of trouble. I can't imagine what you'd do if you bought a house." Actually, the large purchases are the easiest to handle with this system of separate ownership. The terms of property ownership are specified in the title to the house. As a married couple, you may own property jointly or as tenants-in-common. Joint tenancy implies an undivided half-ownership by each partner with the right of survivorship. (If your spouse dies, you automatically inherit the property by operation of law.) Most real estate sales people recommend joint ownership to married couples for this reason. But joint tenancy has consequences. You lose your right to will your property to whomever you wish, and the surviving spouse could possibly save estate taxes if he/she were the will beneficiary rather than the co-owner. In divorce, the right of ownership is not specified, and the house—as part of the shared property—is subject to the laws of the state. However, a divorce will, in most cases, change the co-ownership from joint tenancy with rights of survivorship to ownership as tenants-in-common.

Ownership as tenants-in-common permits a married couple to specify the share (in percent) of property—and, if desired, the piece of the property (the grounds, the first floor, etc.)—owned by each partner. If one partner dies, his share can be willed to the surviving spouse. In divorce, a settlement can be based on the value of each share of the property, because it had been clearly identified beforehand.

Because the law is in flux and the Revenue Act of 1978 has passed, a lawyer or professional financial planner might help you determine the form of ownership best suited to your needs.

Let us assume you are using the Separate Property System and you want to buy a house for $50,000 in Mill Valley, California. The required cash down payment on the mortgage is $10,000. You and your partner both want a half interest in the house as tenants-in-common and each agrees to pay half the monthly payments. After you have both placed $5,000 in escrow and the title clears, the house is yours. Your title will be recorded as follows:

Grant Deed: By this instrument, dated March 4, 1977, for valuable consideration, Joseph King and Melitta M. King, his wife, hereby grant to Jack Smith and Jill Armstrong, husband and wife, each an undivided one-half interest as separate property, as Tenants-in-Common, the following described real property in the State of California, County of Marin, City of Mill Valley. . . .

Title companies, real estate salespeople, and bankers may not understand why you want ownership as tenants-in-common. But this is a practical and sensible arrangement for people who buy real estate and don't buy Blessed Assumptions.

A Tax Tip

The tax laws are subject to change but, as of this writing, many couples pay extra taxes each year simply because they are married. Marital status should be irrelevant to the amount of tax a couple pays, since taxes are based on assumptions about the nature of the marital relationship which may or may not be true. A couple that conforms to the husband-as-breadwinner-and-wife-as-dependent-homemaker concept will find that marriage brings a tax-saving. However, an employed husband and an employed wife may be dismayed to discover that they would be better off as two single taxpayers than as a married couple.

A married person pays different tax sums according to whether the return is filed as "married, filing jointly" or as "married, filing separately." Generally, a married person who files a separate tax return pays more taxes. With the Separate Property System, you can file your return either way. A simple way to determine the most advantageous way to file is for each partner to compute the percentage of his or her income of the joint gross income. Use this figure to calculate the tax you would pay if filing a joint return and compare this tax to the tax you would pay using a "Married, Filing Separately" return. You will then know if you win or lose tax dollars by filing jointly. Depending on the complexity of your fiscal situation, the advice of a Certified Public Accountant may be helpful.

Cozy Contracts

You can contract with your spouse to use the Separate Property System. Think of this: If you don't decide how you want to arrange your finances, the state will—and already has. A contract can be a simple written statement or a document prepared by a lawyer. The contract between my husband and myself was written by a lawyer (and is presented in Chapter 14). The fact that you have a contract will quiet unenlightened people when they object to your independent financial functioning.

You will probably never show the contract to anyone. You will probably never use it. But, as in business, a written contract will strengthen the understanding. Your contract with your spouse about money and a written will are the two most important pieces of paper needed as statements of your position in the marriage.

A happy marriage is likely to remain a happy marriage for couples who maintain control over their own money. Independence within marriage nourishes the soul and actually enhances feelings of love. More than a lot of other couples, you can count on staying together, because money won't matter.

CHAPTER **8**

Your Freedom

"I'm jist a girl who cain't say no, I'm in a turrible fix. . . ."

THE ONE AREA OF RESPONSIBILITY that stimulates more discourse and negotiation than any other between married partners is housework. In this area, resentments often surface and can result in deadlocks.

But solutions are available to those people willing to examine their options. How you spend your time is important— whether you are Hannah Homemaker, Carrie Career, or Judy the Juggler. For whichever alternative you choose, dirt shows no regard.

In many marriages, housework is assumed to be the wife's job. The husband supports her to do this work as part of an implicit marriage agreement. She works in the home to keep her children and husband happy. Knowing that she has provided the family with a clean place to live and that she has "done it all herself" may be a source of satisfaction. Appreciation of family members for her efforts to make the house into a home can be rewarding, but is it enough?

Have you ever heard the complaint, "When I have the time, I don't have the money. And when I have the money, I don't have the time"? This accurately reflects the relationship between two valuable commodities: Time equals money.

The time spent toiling in the house is worth money. According to a recent time-motion task study,* the work of the homemaker is worth from $5,000 to $7,500 a year. (The younger the children at home, the higher the value placed on the labor.) Tasks performed by the average worker at home include that of nursemaid, dietician, food-buyer, dishwasher, housekeeper, launderer, seamstress, practical nurse, maintenance person, gardener, and chauffeur. As an alternative to "doing it yourself," your time can be exchanged for dollar income and that can be exchanged for household services.

Many women leave positions with low pay and little opportunity for advancement to become housewives. The old job is traded for the housewife job that also offers no opportunity for advancement, but possibly offers greater job satisfaction. Spending money is dependent on the husband's income, and if his income is likely to increase, staying at home is a better deal than functioning in a lackluster job.

Most women can make more money outside than inside the home. Most men, though, make more money than women. One reason male salaries may be higher than female salaries is because employers traditionally assume men "need" the money to support a family. Assuming one partner should manage the household, the marriage partner with the lowest-dollar earning power gets the housework job. This self-perpetuating

* "The American Woman: To Many, Happiness Still Means Staying at Home," Special Section/Women: *U.S. News & World Report*, vol. 79, no. 23, December 8, 1975, p. 64.

"Catch-22" situation keeps the woman at home in charge of housework.

Persons in the important homemaker role have low occupational status in our culture, not because the job is considered insignificant, but because the work is usually performed by women. As women gain dollar earning power and as men enter homemaking, the job of homemaker will gain status. (When men were secretaries and bank tellers, these jobs were prestigious training grounds for executive positions. But when performed by women, these same jobs lost status and became career dead ends.)

Your Choice

The married woman's status as homemaker is a Blessed Assumption founded on a fixed marital structure. Since the structure of marriage is flexible, however, the role of homemaker is up for grabs. There are choices: You can be the homemaker, or your spouse can be the homemaker (in the two-career marriage), or you can both be half-homemaker. Or you can hire a homemaker (in the three-career marriage, explained later). Your time can either be traded for dollar income or used to provide household services. You decide what will make you the happiest and what to you makes the most sense.

BUT I HAVE NO CHOICE

Some homemakers say they would prefer a job outside the home, but can't get one "because——————" (you complete the rest of the sentence). You can do whatever you *want* to do, so there are no excuses for your career never flourishing because you majored in Greek and there were no jobs during the Depression for Greek majors (and that's why you still can't get a job). Certainly, there is more difficulty finding jobs in some occupations than in others. But reevaluate your talents, explore your potential, and persist.

BUT MY HUSBAND WANTS ME AT HOME

If staying at home makes you unhappy, yet your husband wants you at home, question his reasons. Ask him if your happiness is not more important than his objections. His happiness should not depend on *what* you do, but on the fact that what you do makes you happy.

The Two-Career Marriage Choice

You may say, "But I'm a housewife and I like it." Homemaking is a respectable career choice for anyone, male or female, provided that the need for independence is recognized within this basically dependent situation. The housewife is granted support on the grounds that she is married. But in other work roles, payment is acknowledged for the tasks performed. If she were not working at home, the housewife could be working outside the home and be considered self-supporting. How often, when housewives have been asked, "What do you do?" have they replied, "Nothing." The fallacy is obvious. The homemaker performs "unpaid" work and because this work demands all her time she (he) is unable to perform work outside the home for which she (he) would be paid. Her support is not recognized for work performed, but rather as an assumed obligation of the husband. Ironically, many women who are homemakers after marriage could make considerable money outside the home and more than offset the cost of services needed to maintain the household operation. In these circumstances, the occupation of housewife becomes a luxury few families can afford.

There is no reason for you to give up your job as housewife if you gain enjoyment from it. However, you could realize greater personal satisfaction if your work was compensated for (yes, in dollars). Your "boss" is your husband. You are dependent on him for almost *everything*. Unless you are a rare person, you are bound to resent this dependency and he, at times, may resent his responsibility to you.

If you are a housewife, all income is probably your husband's earned salary. Because of the services you provide, he is better able to perform at his job and to relax in the comfort of his home and in the knowledge that the children are being reared with loving care. If you both desire this arrangement, then he must acknowledge your contribution to his earnings (time, psychological support, keeping the home pleasant so as not to interfere with his work, etc.), as well as the mutually beneficial services you provide to the family. If you spend your time working, you should get paid.

COMPENSATING THE COOK

"Woman's work" had a market value in earlier centuries when fathers were paid for the loss of their daughters' services. Today the worth of these household services is usually recognized only at the time of divorce, when the wife who interrupted her career for the marriage is compensated by alimony. Get paid during your marriage and avoid having to be awarded severance pay by a court!

Your husband may think an "allowance" is all you need. An allowance is a charitable gift. You should both agree that any money received out of your husband's paycheck is for your work contribution. You are exchanging your time for his money. He is not granting you a favor. By trading some of his income for some of your time, the family unit can function harmoniously and you can achieve independence.

Payment for your work at home may seem silly until you try it. Negotiate a salary with your "boss" by asking for a percentage of his salary. Your own earned money is important. Your head will feel great—you will feel a freedom and worth not realized when you were a dependent housewife. You may decide instead to settle for a fixed income (with an expected yearly raise), but asking for a percentage of your husband's salary has a hidden advantage. Especially if the prospect of making money excites you, you may find some added incentive to see that he does well in his job because the more money he makes, the more money you get! In this way, your support as homemaker, helpmate, and wife counts (in dollars). You will love the fact that you need not "beg" for every little item you want from your husband and your husband will be forced to not take your job for granted. You will both be working toward his success. If you can agree to a 50–50 split on his income (which I recommend), then you also have the opportunity to negotiate all joint purchases with equal bargaining power. Women (or men) who prefer the home life can also use the Separate Property System and keep money separate.

Your job as homemaker revolves around family needs. Because of the nature of the job, when everyone else is playing, you're working. But that doesn't mean you never get a chance to play. By careful allocation of your time, you can structure your job around your family to allow leisure and work time—just like anybody else who works. Give yourself an eight-hour workday. Perhaps you can work four hours in the morning and four hours in the evening, giving yourself the afternoon for fun. Suit yourself. On weekends your husband can pitch in to help you with your housekeeping chores or, if family demands create major workloads on weekends, take off two weekdays. Value yourself. Don't say that you do not work because you enjoy being a housewife. Consider yourself one of the lucky few who enjoy what they do for a living.

Despite the recognized relationship between time and money in the business world, time wasted by the homemaker is not considered a national issue. Women have a low regard for the value of their own and other women's time. My involvement with "women's groups" which always started an hour or more late made me realize this sad truth.

The homemaker can change this and improve her situation by viewing herself as manager of a business. Women at home tend to have a day full of interruptions. Bringing together a group of "busy executives" is easier than bringing together a group of "busy homemakers." The woman-at-home has a job with undefined hours and a telephone that isn't always covered. Whoever heard of being able to conduct a business like that? Your home is where you work, and it should have the same amenities as any other business. To increase your happiness and thereby the quality of your marriage and to let your husband know what he's paying for, here are guidelines to help organize your work:

1. Write your own job description. Include all tasks for which you are responsible and projects requiring long-range planning. Identify the hours you plan to work.
2. Every week, prepare a schedule of what you want to accomplish. Be realistic. It may take a while to discover how to manage your time, so do not get discouraged if at first you don't accomplish everything on your list. Also, schedule your hours of free time. If you were working in an office, your free time would be evenings and weekends. For the homemaker, the opposite may be true. So fit in rest and relaxation when you can. For example, if your evenings are spent fixing dinner, bathing the children, and preparing meals for the next day, schedule three morning hours for household tasks (shopping, cleaning, repair calls, and so forth) and take four

hours in the afternoon for play (reading, relaxing in the sun, or visiting an art gallery).

3. To the degree possible, perform "like tasks" in the same block of time. For example, do all the major pre-meal preparation chores at one time. Do not spread housecleaning throughout the day. Return all your phone calls at the same time. (See below.)

4. Odd as this may sound, you—the woman-at-home—need a way to receive telephone messages when you're not there. This eliminates time wasted waiting for calls. Get a telephone answering machine or hire an answering service. How else will you know what calls you missed and how you can be more organized and get on with the business of running a house? The cost of an answering machine is well worth the investment (about $100, new). Your husband would not think of asking his associates to run a business without telephone coverage, yet this same man may ask you to run a house efficiently without a budget, pay, and a way to receive messages.

You may discover that you need more than forty hours a week to do the job. If so, maybe other family members will help when they see your workload written on paper. You may also want to choose some of the solutions to housework suggested below for the "three-career marriage."

The Three-Career Marriage Choice

When husband and wife both choose a career outside the home, there is no homemaker. Happiness in these marriages is precipitously balanced according to a couple's ability to resolve the conflict between the demands of home life and devotion to career. Life can be hectic for those working couples who attempt to absorb the work of the missing home-maker, and the importance of housework is dramatically re-vealed: It is another full-time job, and two people cannot easily meet the demands of three careers.

One could spend a whole life cleaning and never finish, because things around a house always collect dirt, get out of order, and need organization. Once in a while, housework can be fun and good exercise, but it can also be an excessive demand on the marriage. Without a wife in the traditional role, salaried couples struggle to make up for this lack by cooking TV dinners, doing laundry at midnight, and shop-ping for food on weekends.

This is the problem: You both share living space and that living space gets dirty. Spending your time and energy at the end of a workday or on the weekend to clean house and run errands is not fun. And you both deserve to have fun.

This is the solution to the problem: Having traded your time for salaried dollars, buy service. Put yourself in the role of the traditional husband. He supports someone he loves and she provides household services. Now you could *both* support someone (love not required) to provide household services and avoid running yourselves ragged.

In this way, you do not have to spend your only free time together cleaning the house. Working couples must experi-ment in this area until they reach a mutually satisfactory solu-tion. And if you don't like housework, both of you can forget it! There *are* solutions.

THE "I HATE HOUSEWORK" SOLUTION

The simplest solution is to trade your dollars for service. Since your marriage does not reflect the Blessed Assumptions, you cannot expect it to provide the traditional arrangements. Start out with a once-a-week housecleaner for only a few hours each week. Then, while you are skiing or lying on the beach together, think about the time you saved for enjoyment instead of cleaning.

Before hiring your housecleaner, make a list of the chores to be accomplished and decide upon the level of cleanliness you desire. If one partner is meticulous and the other doesn't care, compromise. If you use the Separate Property System, the housecleaning cost is an expense equally shared. The amount to be spent, however, can be negotiated.

You may decide that cleaning only certain rooms is important. For example, my husband and I decided that only the kitchen and bathrooms needed a good regular cleaning, so we hired someone to concentrate on those rooms and, if time remained, to attend to other cleaning details. I will never forget the wonderful feeling of coming home from work and, for the first time, finding an immaculately clean house.

There are probably some chores that you *like* to do. I like to water the plants and I love oiling furniture. My husband likes to wash windows. These chores, therefore, never appear on our housecleaning list. One task I like to do, but always forget, is to wind the old grandfather clock; so that task *is* on the list. Alongside the list of chores and tasks to be accomplished, specify the regularity of attention needed. The vacuuming might be done every week, but the silver polished only once every six months. (See sample list of chores on the next page.)

The responsibility for this list should not be shared (but do consult with your spouse). One partner should take the responsibility for the list and the other partner should take another responsibility—such as finding the housekeeper or keeping track of the supply of cleaning materials. Rates for housecleaning vary by neighborhood, and what you can afford to spend on it depends on your income and how much you value your time together.

SAMPLE HOUSECLEANING LIST

EVERY WEEK	EVERY MONTH	EVERY SIX MONTHS
Empty wastebaskets	Spot-clean walls	Scrub bathroom walls
Vacuum entire house	Wax bathroom floor	Polish fixtures
Shake out white rug	Clean china cabinet	Clean kitchen oven
Clean entire bathroom: (toilet bowl, mirror, enamel surfaces, bathtub)	Wax kitchen floor	Clean doors to den
	Clean refrigerator	Shampoo rug where needed
Clean entire kitchen (sink), and vacuum small carpet	Clean garbage container	
Clean coffee table in living room		
Put bedspreads on line		
Wind grandfather clock		

Another alternative to the weekly (or every-other-week) housecleaner is the professional cleaning service. One couple I know, parents of two small children, have contracted with a cleaning service to send a crew once a month to do a thorough cleaning, including washing the walls, waxing the floors, and cleaning the oven.

The biggest obstacle to hiring a housecleaner is usually your own psychological resistance: How do I find someone I can trust? Where should I look?

Hiring a housecleaner is like hiring anyone for any job—you take a chance, trusting to your instincts. The best source is a friend who can recommend someone. You can also find housecleaners through high school and college employment offices (for part-time work) and through ads in your local paper. Always interview anyone before hiring her or him and always check references. Generally, I've had no problem of the sort most homedwellers fear—no one has ever been inter-

ested in my treasures. Once I even hired a housecleaner without
following one of my two basic rules—I did not personally interview her, except by phone (although she did have excellent references). She cleaned our house for six months and
we never met during that time. We exchanged notes, and
every week she opened the door with a housekey which was
lodged in a secret hiding place. Her work was excellent. One
day she left a note saying she had decided to move to Hawaii.
My husband and I, curious to meet her, invited her to dinner.
She was delightful and we were sorry to see her go.

You will find that you can trust most people. Your fears of
thievery are probably unfounded and the value of your
possessions to others overrated.

Some people claim it is not "right" for an outsider to clean
one's home. "You should clean your own dirt," they say.
Viewing the job as menial and low-paying, these people de-
grade the employee. Pay the going rate, pay a good rate, and
you will feel no guilt. Housecleaning is an honorable profession. It's a good job: you're your own boss, the hours are
often flexible, there's a freedom not found in other jobs (you
can whistle while you work) and if you appreciate fine things,
you can enjoy working in some lovely homes. The housecleaner, however, does not have the traditional protections
granted regular employees (which is the case for all self-
employed people). If you are a person who makes the decision to clean the house yourself because you believe hiring
help is exploiting someone, think of the fact that you are
downgrading someone else and taking away their job as well.

When you find the right person, give him or her a starting date and establish a regular schedule—for example, "every
other Monday for four hours." Provide whatever is needed for
the jobs you want done, and, whenever possible, be ac-
commodating concerning the housecleaner's preferences.
(One of our housecleaners wanted to use a particular brand
of biodegradable cleanser which we were happy to supply.)

Make the job pleasant for your housecleaner and, as in any business, problems will be reduced and the turnover rate will be low. Every six months or every year, assuming you are pleased with her/his performance, a raise would be appropriate.

Occasionally, you may find someone who does not meet your expectations. If you feel you have explained the tasks clearly, but still the quality of the work lags, dismiss the housecleaner. Simply say: "We will not need you next week. We've decided not to have the house cleaned for a while and we'll call you if we need the work done again."

Do not try to explain why or train the person to clean your way. (You are not an expert on cleaning.) You can tell a housecleaner what to clean but you cannot tell her or him how to clean. You wouldn't hire a secretary and tell her or him how to type. Instead, find a person who does meet your standards.

THE "PARTNERS IN GRIME" SOLUTION

If you are a working couple with an average income of less than the going rate for housecleaners, you may decide that even a part-time housecleaner is a luxury you cannot afford. In that case, you will have to distribute the workload between you.

First, decide the tasks necessary to perform and list them on paper. Is there anything on the list that you or your partner like to do? With the remaining tasks, either draw straws or negotiate and settle. Try to arrange a time (once a week) when you will do these chores. Set a time limit—perhaps three hours. You'll be amazed how much two people can accomplish. When we used this solution and were tired after completing the chores, we rewarded ourselves with a favorite treat—ice cream.

Another alternative I've found very successful is to assign

each partner specific rooms in the house. The agreement is that you will both maintain your assigned rooms but can clean at your convenience as often as is necessary. List the room assignment and tasks if you prefer, as shown on the sample "Partners in Grime" worksheet. Occasionally, one partner may fall down on the job. Agree to be flexible, but also agree that one's partner has the right to "nag" if one slips. If it is not your room, do not clean it. Eventually, the rooms *will* get cleaned.

Lacking the courage to hire a housekeeper when we started our marriage, my husband and I attempted to do our own housework. I did the cooking while he set the table and made the salad. We shared the loading and unloading of the the dishwasher. We discovered, though, that our most workable arrangement was one of not sharing chores. The best arrangement we've ever had is the one we now use: He does *all* the cooking. I do *all* the cleaning up. I hated being tied to a time when I had to prepare dinner, although I didn't mind having dinner prepared on time. Cleaning up is great for me because I can do it whenever I please and I often put it off until late evening (my least productive business hours). Once in a while, when he's going to be home very late, I do the cooking and then he cleans. We also have nights called "Each Man for Himself"—meaning we each prepare our own dinner and clean up after ourselves. This occurs when I want to eat chicken livers, which he refuses to eat, or when he wants to eat hot Mexican food, which disturbs my digestion.

Another housework plan—successful for people with children—is to use a checklist. Every household task is listed on a sheet of paper and hung in a convenient spot—say, in the kitchen. The names of all household members are written across the top of the page and each task checked upon completion. Tasks are designated weekly, so every week a new list must be drawn up. This approach requires a manager (prob-

"PARTNERS IN GRIME" WORKSHEET

ROOM	PERSON	FREQUENCY
Kitchen:	Jane	
Clean countertop		once/week
Vacuum rug		once/week
Clean window		once/month
Clean refrigerator		once/month
Bathroom:	Ralph	
Clean tub		once/week
Clean sink, toilet		once/week
Clean fixtures		once/week
Wax floor		once/month
Replace bath mat		once/week
Living Room:	Jane	
Vacuum rug		once/week
Dust		once/week
Clean walls		once/3 months
Hallway:	Ralph	
Damp-mop floor		once/week
Dust pictures		once/2 weeks

Etc.

ably you), so take that into account and try to switch the management responsibility from time to time so that you don't become the constant taskmaster.

Give yourselves time to find the best arrangement to suit your personalities. Invest in time-saving equipment. One appliance that is indispensable for the working couple is the dishwasher. You can get a used portable dishwasher for as little as $50.

Cleanliness is relative. What is dirty to you may be clean to me. Do your own housework only if hiring a housecleaner would create financial distress. Cleanliness, said to be next to godliness, might also contribute to marital happiness.

What do you do when your spouse refuses to share either the physical or fiscal responsibility for house chores? You do nothing, and eventually the issue will surface. It is human nature to resist work one doesn't want to do as long as one can, and often a partner will try to "wait you out" because he (she) believes you will eventually do the necessary cleaning. Your tolerance will be tested, but the "do nothing" approach will make a point. When your partner complains about a dirty house, ask "What should *we* do to correct the situation?" Another approach: Clean the house for several weeks, during which time your partner will learn to enjoy a clean place. Then stop. Wait for the complaint. There may be a childish testing of wills—be prepared for the battle. Your freedom is worth the contest.

My husband and I at times do our own housework and at other times hire outside help. Our solutions to housekeeping problems are geared to fit our needs. You, too, should discuss and experiment until you find the arrangement that is right for you and your partner. And then be willing to change again. If your solution works beautifully for one month and then falls apart, solve the problem again. The more experience you get solving these housework problems, the better able you will be to handle other problems. You will discover that solutions always exist and can be found by examining the options open to free people.

CHAPTER 9

Your Own Space

"Plen'y of room to swing a rope! Plen'y of heart and plen'y of hope. . . ."

THE SUBJECT OF LIVING SPACE is ignored in most books on marriage. In the traditional marital arrangement an assumption is made about living space that may not be geared to maximum happiness. This assumption is that everything must be shared—the bedroom, the bathroom, almost every room in the house. But many homes could be much happier if each person, children as well as adults, had his or her own space.

Your own space can be a cellar workshop or a room to plan projects or to do anything else you want. It can be a physical space—a place to be messy, to be orderly—or it can be a space in time in which to meditate.

A Part of Being Together

Living together and sharing space robs an individual of the opportunity to be alone. To lose your own private moments is to lose a personal freedom—a freedom you probably had when you were single. Women at home with children become acutely aware of the need for a space or time free from the clatter of children and of home responsibilities. One woman I know, the mother of three small children, has set aside a room for jewelry-making to retreat to for one or two hours a day. The room is off limits to the rest of the family. Another woman hires a babysitter so that she can leave the house for several hours each day. She claims her "time out" keeps her sane.

Shared living space infringes on your property as well as your privacy. Sharing a closet with a closet-hog mate can be a daily irritant. Communal bathrooms, liked shared closets, can also create disharmony. Conversations around bathrooms are reduced to: "Get out, you're taking too long." "Who left the toothpaste uncapped?" "Keep your dirty hands off my clean towel." Such charming exchanges between lovers! These are only slight irritations, but slight chronic irritations spawn major battles.

Each person needs a different amount of space in his life. During the first years of marriage, space needs may not seem as great as in later years, when you can become crowded by too much togetherness. Following are suggestions you may wish to consider for achieving space for yourself in marriage. Every suggestion offered has worked for someone.

Separateness

THE SEPARATE BEDROOM

According to our cultural mores, attitudes, and sexual beliefs, the bedroom is the one room of the house a married couple *must* share. It is commonly believed that any couple not sharing a bedroom must be unhappy.

But the bedroom can be both a battleground and a place

of pleasure. Couples who can't agree on room temperature and the number of blankets needed for sleeping comfort, or on the hour for arising in the morning know the misery caused by bedroom-sharing. Nevertheless, few of these couples opt for separate bedrooms.

One New Hampshire couple I know argued for years over the temperature of the bedroom. He liked a cold room and insisted on fresh air even when it was snowing. She preferred warmth, so she purchased a sleeping bag, but still had to put up with dressing in a cold room. It never occurred to them that separate bedrooms might be the answer to their problem.

As newlyweds, my husband and I slept in a king-sized bed. My husband preferred the sheets tucked taut; I preferred them loose and free. He arose at six every morning and wanted me in bed when he went to sleep at ten every night. Since I was a student, this schedule was unsuited to my routine (not to mention my biorhythm). For a year we argued over the early bedtime. He wanted a full night's sleep and I wanted to work late into the night. He woke me when he rose early and I woke him when I went to bed late. Then the thought struck me: "Why don't we just have separate bedrooms?"

When we moved from a small apartment to a large house, I suggested the change in sleeping arrangements. At first my husband objected strongly, but after discussing it further we decided that if it did not work out, we could always go back to the old way. The first week I felt lonely without him beside me, but gradually a new sense of freedom emerged. We *both* found we preferred our own rooms.

Now my husband would not think of returning to the shared bedroom. He loves his privacy. A special collection of favorite books is spread on the floor by his bedside; he has the room organized the way *he* likes it to suit *his* convenience. We no longer argue or are annoyed with one another because of lost sleep. And our sex life has actually improved. It is much more fun to rendezvous in each other's bedroom! Our physical awareness and sensitivity to each other has increased, since we are not numbed by a physical closeness that has become routine.

When I suggested this arrangement to a male friend who complained about sleep lost because of his wife's snoring, he said, "Now that's going too far. My wife is going to be in my bed. You don't expect me to give up sex."

There is almost always an association made between sleeping in the same bed and sex, and, admittedly, there is a sexual convenience resulting from bed-sharing. But unless you're having sexual relations eight hours every night, there is no reason to share a bed during that whole time. There is nothing sexually exciting about sleeping with someone who snores, who tosses and turns, who likes the room cool when you like it warm, or who wakes you when you want to sleep. All these are negative influences on what should be a pleasurable experience—in bed together, making love. Also, missing your partner can be healthy for the relationship. When you do see each other, you will be more likely to touch. And when you *are* in bed together, the encounter should be more exciting. My husband and I "visit" each other every night—sometimes in his room, sometimes in mine. We talk and discuss the day's events. Before we part, we hug and kiss. In the morning, we greet each other with a warm embrace. Isn't that the way it should be? The quality of the time we spend together has been enhanced by eliminating combat from the bedroom. Two non-communicative and tired bodies can dull the most exciting physical relationships.

You will be absolutely amazed at the change for the better that separate bedrooms can make in your marriage. Until you try this new lifestyle you may never realize how much resentment you may have harbored over compromised bedroom habits. And if you don't like the arrangement, you can always return to the shared bed. That's the fun of experimenting with

your marriage. When you find the best arrangement for yourselves—no matter how unconventional (or conventional)—
you both have won. That's success.

THE SEPARATE APARTMENT

One San Francisco couple, George and Anne Feiler, needed
more breathing space in their relationship. George, who had
been single for thirty-five years, felt stifled by seeing one
person every day. Although he loved Anne, he felt the marriage was closing in on him.

Their solution was to find separate apartments in the same
building—one on the first floor, one on the third. Anne was
delighted by the prospect of decorating her own place and
by her new freedom.

"I live by my own rhythm: waking, sleeping, and eating
when it pleases me; cleaning or not cleaning; having noise or
quiet. This freedom is my treasure." *

After three years they stated that distance from each other
allowed them to know themselves better and enabled them to
share more of their inner selves.

If you live in a large house, you and your partner might
consider having separate living quarters on a different floor
or in another section of the house. Many parents have improved relationships with their children by giving them their
own space in an attic or semi-attached structure. Why not
allow yourselves the same freedom?

Couples must find the right distance and space arrangement for themselves. For us, the separate apartment was "too
far," the shared bedroom was "too close," but the separate
bedroom was "just right."

---

* George and Anne Feiler, "Two Views of a Marriage," *California
Living (San Francisco Sunday Examiner and Chronicle)*, January 23,
1977, pp. 10–13.

THE SEPARATE VACATION

There are other ways to get your own space besides moving your furniture to a separate room or apartment. One of the happiest couples I've ever met said that the secret to their successful marriage was separate vacations. He went camping in the desert and she went swimming in Hawaii, but not at the same time. The experience of being home alone (while the other travelled) was liberating and enjoyable.

To me, vacation means lying on the beach, swimming, spending evenings poolside, and shopping during the coolest part of the afternoon. To my husband, a vacation means adventure—travelling to and exploring new places. It is fun for him to spend the day touring in a car.

When we attempted to satisfy the vacation preferences of both of us, we compromised by going to a place with a beach that also offered ample opportunity for exploration. I spent more time than I wanted in the car and he was limited to distances of a day's travel time.

My husband's best vacation was probably the one he took alone. He travelled by motorcycle from San Francisco to Fairbanks, Alaska, loving every minute. I was included in the trip even though I wasn't there. He called me every night and described the beauty he witnessed en route. It was exciting to share his adventure and delight while I sat in my comfortable chair by the telephone. If I had been sitting on the rear seat of his motorcycle I would have been miserable, spoiling his good time. We both won.

Deciding to exercise my option on the separate vacation as well, I flew to Palm Springs. Checking into the hotel by myself gave me a strange feeling. Sitting alone by the pool was not boring the first hour. But then prowling men discovered I was alone. I learned as a married woman what I had known when I was single: A woman travelling alone can expect unwanted attention. After four days of trying to have a good time by myself, I cancelled my reservation and flew home, happier than ever to see my husband.

However, the separate vacation can be successful. Palm Springs may not have been a wise choice for me. And if I go again, I will bring a friend, someone who also loves the sun and poolside lolling.

Removed from everyday surroundings, one may gain new perspectives and insights. The separate vacation is one way to achieve your own space. I recommend it—some of the time, but not all the time.

THE SEPARATE WORK WEEK

Circumstances sometimes force one partner to move to a different city. The result can often be surprisingly beneficial to the relationship.

Dave was offered an excellent job opportunity in Modesto, a small California city two hundred miles away. Although fearful of being apart, Dave and his wife Kay decided that the most sensible way to handle the situation was for him to work in Modesto during the weekdays and to return home on weekends. With this arrangement, Kay, a lawyer, could keep her practice and their children could continue going to school with their friends. To their amazement, the separation put new life into their marriage. Fifteen years of being together had made them complacent; now when Dave returns home there is excitement in seeing each other.

THE JOB THAT SEPARATES

For most couples, living in separate states is "too far away." But what happens if you are happily situated in your career and your husband is offered a fantastic job opportunity in another state? What should you do? This is a difficult decision to make and one that should be discussed *before* it happens.

The alternatives are clear: You can leave your job and move to the new state with your husband; your husband can reject the offer; or you can stay where you are and keep your desirable job, while your husband moves into his new apartment in a different state.

The decision will pivot around whether or not location is more important than career and whose career comes first.

My husband and I faced this problem when his company asked him to transfer to Boston, Massachusetts. I did not want to move. I was finishing my dissertation in California at the time and viewed this interruption in our lives as something that could cost me several years of graduate work. He was not anxious to live in Boston either, but the career opportunity was tempting.

We weighed the alternatives. Every time I thought of moving to Boston, I thought about the candidates I knew who had postponed work on their doctorates for similar reasons and never resumed it. Then I had an idea: My friend Marge could live with me while my husband worked in Boston. My husband and I could meet every three months or during semester breaks, and perhaps in another two years he would be transferred back to Oakland. He wasn't enthusiastic about my idea and searched for another solution. He finally decided that he would try to find a job in San Francisco as good as the one offered in Boston. Two weeks before his scheduled departure, he came home with the good news. He had found another job—an even better one—in San Francisco.

As a result of this crisis and because we knew it would happen again (I was later offered an interesting position in Hawaii), we decided to place location over career. Since we both love living in the San Francisco Bay Area, we agreed that our careers would revolve around our favorite city. This decision has saved us grief and has not seriously hampered our careers. We also agreed that if a position is offered to one of us and it means relocation, we will move only if we *both* agree we want the change.

Other couples have discovered ingenious solutions to the transfer problem. I know a woman sociologist who "commutes" to Northwestern University every semester and returns to San Francisco during academic breaks. She is taking advantage of a significant professional opportunity while her husband maintains his job in San Francisco.

If you and your partner decide to place location before career, select a city you both love. *Then* look there for that career opportunity. Remember that you probably can find a job or pursue your career living in or near almost any large city in the United States if you are persistent and inventive.

My sister and her husband are a case in point. They decided they wanted to live in Florida. Most of their married life was spent transferring from place to place—New York to Michigan to Ohio. They were both tired of cold weather and snow, so he responded to newspaper employment ads for jobs in warmer climates. When nothing satisfactory turned up after two years, he left the corporation and, without jobs (but with savings), they packed their bags and arrived on the Gulf Coast of Florida. One month later she had a job with a medical firm. Two months later he opened his own business. Now they are both happy and as free as flamingos. Their career ladders changed, but they are satisfied the change is for the better. In a location they love, they are both pursuing new careers.

Growing relationships need room.

CHAPTER **10**

Children: A Special Issue

"I'm jist a fool when lights are low. . . ."

MARRIAGES CAN BE DIVIDED into two kinds—those with and those without children. Perpetuating the species is a major life decision. But as wonderful as children may seem, they can be a stress on any marriage.

Married people often feel pressured by relatives and society to have children. Yet the decision to marry and the decision to procreate are separate decisions.

People delight in having children for different reasons. Children can be an augmentation of one's ego or an extension of the family bloodline. In some cultures children are valued as a source of labor. In our culture, parents hope their children will be a source of joy and will enrich the love and sharing in their lives. Many parents also expect their children to comfort and aid them in their golden years.

Seldom neutral, parents are either exhilarated or disappointed by their children. Those whose children are professionals or bear beautiful grandchildren are proud parents. Those with children who have become drug addicts, delinquents, or school dropouts are worried and apologetic. The paean "Children are wonderful" is sung mostly by the parents with children who have turned out as their parents hoped, or better.

Having children is, in some ways, like playing a game of roulette. In this game of chance, your marriage can be enriched—or intolerably strained; your days can be filled with joy—or with disappointment. You can become a more dynamic person—or a stifled, frustrated one. Before you spin the wheel, evaluate carefully the risks to your physical well-being, your person, and your marriage.

Taking a Chance on Love

Parenthood requires a physical and an emotional commitment by both parents to a child. But, why is it that women carry the lion's share of work and concern when it comes to children?

THE PHYSICAL RISK

A mother generally feels a greater responsibility toward the offspring than the father does because she has had to make a greater personal investment to start with—nine months' worth. At some inner psychological level a mother has had to say, "I am willing to put my life on the line for this child." Her husband has had to say, "I am willing to be responsible." From the beginning, her commitment is greater than his, because pregnancy, childbirth, and motherhood, which are romantically glorified in our culture, can threaten a woman's health and happiness. Almost all women suffer some physical disorder during their pregnancy—varicose veins, lower back pain, hemorrhoids, and dental problems are only a few of the most common. Minor distress, brought about by dizziness, headaches, edema, and "morning sickness" (vomiting), can last six months or more. In most cases, the woman is physically drained. Some women, on the other hand, find pregnancy a wonderful experience. There is no way to predict which way it will affect any particular woman.

The childbirth experience, too, is unique for each woman. One woman who had a difficult and painful labor recalled how she had dug her fingernails into the hospital plaster, literally climbing the walls in pain. Another recalls the birth of her child as simple and easy. "I hardly felt a thing," she says. Learning how to breathe (à la Lamaze) and being in top physical condition will help ease labor. But there are no guarantees that anaesthesia won't be needed, that a Caesarian section won't have to be performed, or that injuries to mother or child won't result from the baby's difficult trip through the birth canal. Spinal injuries to the mother sometimes occur in a difficult labor. Brain damage can occur to the child. At the very least, most mothers will undergo an episiotomy, which is a standard surgical procedure performed on the vulvar orifice to prevent difficult-to-repair torn tissue. The procedure is considered minor by doctors. To the mother, it may not seem minor, since local anaesthesia is needed before the incision is made, and healing takes weeks.*

At the conclusion of this physical ordeal the mother can be left with what is commonly called "postpartum depression." Sometimes this depression will be serious enough to mar her relationship with her husband, who may not understand why she's not happy. It can take up to two years for a woman's body to fully recover from the hormonal changes and physical stress of childbirth. And the most difficult part of

* Suzanne Arms, "Woman's Body, Woman's Mind: How Hospitals Complicate Childbirth," *Ms.*, vol. 3, no. 11, May 1975, pp. 108–115.

having children is yet to come. It is not the pregnancy or labor or childbirth, but the aftermath—child-rearing—which is a tremendous responsibility and a demanding job.

Usually, the husband does not say, "Well, since you worked so hard to follow your doctor's advice during the pregnancy, and you are tired from the ordeal of delivery, it's now my turn to do some work. I'll take care of the baby." Since a father does not feel the depth of emotion toward a child that the mother does because he is once-removed from the child-bearing process, he is also less likely to be part of the child-rearing process. As in many life situations, commitment comes from emotional and physical investment.

THE EMOTIONAL RISK

The Pleasure: The pleasure derived from children is in watching them grow up, in giving them your affection, and in receiving theirs. Children are also entertaining and delightful, and through them, sometimes, parents can realize lost dreams and relive past fantasies. The world of the child is a wonderful world to share. Becoming a grandparent is the icing on the homemade cake.

The Pain: The pain suffered through children occurs when they do not live up to the parents' ideals. Children can be destructive and menacing. They won't listen to you; they won't share what you want to give. Your love may be despised and rejected. Instead of realizing your dreams, your children may destroy your hopes. They may not understand you. You may not understand them. Crises and conflict can result. Your life may seem compromised; you become sadly disheartened.

Eventually children have to be accepted as individuals who join you in your world and in your home, but who are continually growing more and more independent of you. Their physical appearance may show a likeness to yours, but their spirits are free.

I asked a man who has three grown children what he could tell me about having children. He thought for a moment and commented:

"If most people had a chance to think about it, very few children would be born. Children result from people's naivete. As with marriage, you don't know what having children will be like until you actually have them—there is no predicting.

"Having children and getting married are promoted because parents can't face the fact that they've wasted their whole lives trapped in these circumstances. They want company. Our society does not need a lot of children to sustain itself. There will always be some people who *want* them. Think of the better job we could do with the children we have then."

You guessed it. His children didn't fulfill his dreams. But unlike marital unions, relationships with children who disappoint you cannot be dissolved.

The Big Gamble

Before you decide to have children, consider carefully what is involved: increased responsibility, a change in your maried lifestyle, and a long-term commitment. Further, one person—not two—will generally carry the major share of the child-rearing work.

Be aware too that, though you *can* plan your pregnancy, your child's birth, and its care around your present life goals, people—unenlightened lawmakers and employers, especially —will assume that once you become a mother you will quit your job and stay home caring for your children the rest of your life. Your employer, moreover, may eliminate you from consideration for future advancement once the children come.

In addition, your marital happiness may decline. Dr. Harold

Feldman, of the Department of Human Development and Family Studies at Cornell University, New York, states that in a study of 852 middle-class and upper-class urban couples, "those with children had a significantly lower level of marital satisfaction than those without children. When a couple becomes parents the marital satisfaction declines." *

Children are wearisome. Children are rewarding. As one woman said to me: "What could be more exciting than to watch a child grow?"

ROLLING THE DICE

If you and your partner have different ideas about whether or not children are going to enhance or destroy your marriage, discuss the main issues likely to affect your marital life:

Who will take the major responsibility for the children's care?

How will you keep time for yourselves?

Do you both have the energy to adapt to the changes that children will make in your life?

What are the rewards which you expect children to bring?

My husband and I have chosen not to have children partly because I consider the career of motherhood too difficult for me. (Few persons are truly well suited to this calling.) Children would complicate our present married lifestyle. Neither my husband nor I desire the job of child-rearing. Nor do we want children enough to sacrifice a few of the comforts (such as a quiet house) and freedoms (spur-of-the-moment trips, for example) we now enjoy.

* Harold Feldman, "Changes and Parenthood: A Methodological Design." Unpublished study, Cornell University, Ithaca, N.Y., cited in Shirley L. Radl, *Mother's Day Is Over* (New York: Warner Paperback Library, 1973).

However, many couples find happiness in what we consider work, and what we love to do other couples might consider insignificant. We must be true to ourselves first and choose what we know appeals to us the most.

There are four possible situations concerning desire for children; two appear to be irresolvable.

1. The wife wants the child; the husband does not.
2. The husband wants the child; the wife does not.
3. Both partners want a child.
4. Neither partner wants a child.

Ideally, a child shouldn't be brought into the world unless it is wanted by both partners. If a couple find themselves in situation *1* or *2*, objections may be overcome by a special understanding. Assuming the couple are using the Separate Property System and are willing to give love, the partner desiring the child could assume the major costs and responsibilities for child care. For example:

Situation 1:

You, the woman, want a child; your husband does not. In this case, expenses, arrangements for child care, and so forth will be handled by you. Income will be needed to cover costs, and that means you will probably continue working in your present occupation or find another, maybe part-time, job. Your husband may not want a child because he fears the increased responsibility, expense, and compromise of your time. All these issues should be discussed and, if you wish, can be negotiated and sealed with a contract. This solution may seem strange, but divorced women and single women with children do it all the time.

Situation 2:

Your husband wants a child, you do not. This situation is difficult to resolve; your husband cannot become pregnant. Identify your reasons for not wanting a child. Is it because you do not want a pregnancy to interrupt your career? Or are you afraid to assume the responsibility a child brings? Do you fear the impact that another family member will have upon your lives?

Discuss your feelings with your husband. If you fear responsibility, your husband could offer to assume child-care responsibilities and expenses. However, if you dislike or fear the idea of a pregnancy, there are few options to draw on. In that case, he could adopt a child. He will have to arrange for the child's care and continue his job or work part-time to meet expenses.

Situation 3:

Even if you both desire a child, child care and allocation of money to meet expenses must be discussed. If one partner forgoes a salary to become a full-time homemaker in order to supervise the child, he or she must be guaranteed an income (see Chapter 8). Using the Separate Property System, all child-related costs will become joint expenses. Whatever you do— think, talk, discuss, before you act.

Situation 4:

Couples who don't want children sometimes wish they had something else besides themselves on which to focus. A pet can add another dimension to your relationship without the commitment demanded by a child. By comparison, the pet requires minimal attention and care, yet provides some of the companionship and joy of another living creature.

If you think you might have children someday, caring for and attending to the needs of a pet will offer a glimpse (on a very small scale) of the disruption a child could have on your present way of living.

Regardless of the situation in which you may find yourself, a child is the ultimate responsibility. Are you ready for that?

Child-Care Options

The mother with a career outside the home is faced with seemingly irreconcilable problems. Being a good mother and maintaining equilibrium while working at a full-time job is a balancing act few women can successfully achieve without significant moral support and help from their husbands.

Dual-career stresses are hard to deal with because they involve your feelings about yourself and your view of how others perceive you. However, the management problems are solvable and conquering them will help alleviate the other stresses.

Dr. Judith B. Henderson, Clinical Asst. Professor of Health Psychology at UCSF Medical Center and mother of two, asserts that most mothers are very good managers. She suggests five ways for the employed mother to cope with the demands of children:

1. Live in a place that minimizes the commuting time for both parents.
2. Schedule time for yourself—alone.
3. Keep the baby-sitter during the 5:00 P.M. to 8:00 P.M. transition period after you return home.
4. Employ a baby-sitter when the children are very young and you are home full-time to make your back-to-work transition easier for the child to adjust to—and,
5. Don't feel guilty when your children experience periods of unusual stress—it's not your fault.*

By organizing their schedules and cooperating with outside help, employed couples with children can cope. However, it is not easy and working couples must be willing to trade some of their dollar income for child-care services.

* Judith B. Henderson, from a seminar, "Standing on Your Own Two Feet," The Metropolitan Club, San Francisco, Calif., March 4, 1977.

One career-committed couple with two children worked out a marvelous system to meet their career needs and their children's need for attention. As young executives, both working for different corporations, they devote long days to the office. To make more of their time available to their children, they sold their suburban home and moved to a city location within walking distance of both their offices. Now they can visit the children during their lunch hours. Also, when problems arise they are within easy reach. Their work schedules are arranged around the baby-sitter. Mother goes to her office at 6:00 A.M. and returns home by 5:00 P.M. to relieve the sitter. Father goes to his office at 9:00 A.M., after dressing the children and greeting the sitter, and returns home at 8:00 P.M. Using this system, the parents meet the demands of their respective careers and provide care for their children. The children have an opportunity to spend time alone with each parent every day and they get the benefit of an unrushed and even-tempered mother-substitute all day long. Everyone wins!

Solutions to the problems of child care vary, but they can be categorized as taking place inside or outside the home.

AT-HOME SOLUTIONS

Your child remains in the home. The sitter comes to your house. This solution is very convenient, since there is no need to plan transportation, and when your child is sick, he can stay in his own bed under the watchful eye of the sitter.

The key to making this an ideal solution is finding the right person. The same rules that were applied to hiring a housekeeper should apply to hiring a baby-sitter: advertise, ask for references, interview, and most important, trust your instincts. If you write an ad for the local paper, be businesslike and to the point. Specify your requirements, the ages of your children, and the hours during which the sitter will be needed. Avoid expressions such as "loving, caring person."

When you interview, you can judge whether or not the person is loving and caring or subscribes to your philosophy of life.

Select someone who thinks the way you do and do not be afraid to state your expectations. Ask for two references over the phone and then set a time for a personal interview. In between the phone conversation and the interview appointment you can check references. If the references are not satisfactory, cancel the appointment (you can say you found a neighbor to baby-sit).

The number of hours the sitter is needed will determine your obligation regarding payments toward her Social Security benefits. Check with your Internal Revenue Service office and, if your state requires it, the State Franchise Tax Board, for the necessary forms and detailed information booklets on employing domestic help. Also remember, when filing your income tax returns, that your income bracket may make you eligible to deduct child-care services as a necessary business expense.

Once the sitter is hired, observe how she handles your children. If something she does displeases you, correct her—in private, not in front of the children. A friend of mine overheard her baby-sitter tell her little girl that she was "bad" for pulling down the curtains. The mother explained to the sitter that while she agrees a child should be corrected for wrong behavior, she, the mother, did not believe in ever telling a child that he or she was "bad." The sitter understood and changed her approach.

THE AU PAIR GIRL

Another at-home solution is the hiring of what is commonly referred to as an "au pair girl." Young women, mostly European, will come to the United States to exchange child-care services in your home for room and board, plus a living wage, if you will pay the bill on a one-year tourist visa. These women are interested in seeing America and learning the language. Judging by hearsay, there is about a 50 percent success rate in these arrangements. Many of these women are happy in their American homes and become true mothers' helpers. Others may not be too happy or too helpful. Usually sixteen to twenty years of age, these women, knowing little of the language or of American social protocol, can become more of a hindrance than a help. One woman felt so sorry for her au pair girl, who was depressed and lonely, that she started to cook the girl's meals, buy her clothing, and cater to her needs. Instead of a mother's helper, she gained another child!

The ideal solution appears to be the employment of a mature, reliable, self-sufficient, and supportive nanny, housekeeper, or baby-sitter, who comes to your home daily or who lives in. There are many people who fit that description. You have only to find them.

AWAY-FROM-HOME SOLUTIONS

If you can arrange transportation and want to expose your children to other children, consider the option of the day-care center and the "neighborhood mother."

Day-Care Centers:

Day-care centers have been stigmatized as institutional and sterile. Some are and some are not. Visit the center and decide for yourself. Also, ask your children, if they are old enough, what they think about the center. (After all, they should be consulted. The decision affects them most of all.) Generally, the day-care center will not accept your child on days when he or she is sick, so you must be able to provide a "back-up" on those occasions.

The "Neighborhood Mother":

In some neighborhoods there are women who open their homes to care for the children of working parents. This substitute mother will take your child into her home even when he or she is sick. Usually, she will care for six or seven children, and often includes her own children in the daily activities. Over the course of time, the children will trade toys as well as childhood illnesses. Children usually like this situation because they have a small group of built-in playmates.

One woman takes her son to a neighborhood mother for several hours every day, not because doing so is a solution to her not being at home, but to permit her to have some free time during the day. Further she felt her son was too isolated at home with her all the time. Now he has an opportunity to be with other children.

There are other options for child-care services. Sometimes neighbors and relatives will volunteer to help, but you cannot always rely upon them. Also, a group of homemakers can rotate caring for each others' children; this, however, does not solve the problem of child care for the office worker.

If you make the decision to combine children with career, investigate all these options and any others that seem practical. The earlier you make child-care arrangements, the easier it will be for you to return to your job (if you took a leave of absence) and the easier it will be for your child to accept the idea of being tended to by someone other than you.

Future Family Options

The family structure as we know it may one day be revolutionized by advances in reproductive technology. In the future family, options will be available, not only for fertility control and child-care services, but also for the reproductive methods used to carry the new arrivals. Will there be a day when the fetus' trip through the female birth canal will seem archaic and barbaric? Will there be a day when child care becomes a job for professionals?

We already have the technology for the test-tube baby and

this alternative should be welcomed by all people who believe that increasing human choices will create a better world. In view of the great risk to the mother and to the child inherent in childbirth and the multitude of couples unable to conceive, this option will be greatly appreciated by many.

Childbirth, now, is a strictly female experience. For some, a great one; for others, a horror. Birth outside the womb promises to be healthier for mother and child and will probably encourage parenthood.

You may argue that it's "unnatural." Remember, millions of women have died during delivery and it was not until "unnatural" intervention occurred that many women's lives were saved.

Natural processes are not always beneficial to humankind. Man and women "in nature" are found partly toothless, full of intestinal parasites, and dead before the age of forty. In almost all other parts of the world outside the United States, you will find millions of people, who live without technology in a "natural" setting, with chronic dysentery.

However, the most important effect of relieving woman of the labor of childbirth is social. The major ramification will be that both parents will have the same investment in their children and both will feel equally responsible for child care. Without the close biological association of mother to child, each parent will be on equal footing.

Perhaps I am talking about a phenomenon centuries in the future—or could it be next year? Until childbirth is freed from a woman's womb, the choice between having children and having a career will remain a more compromising one for a woman than for a man because her investment is so great. She cannot have children in today's world without significantly interrupting her physical, social, and psychological condition. Options for methods of reproduction will revolutionize marital, social, and economic relationships—but judging from changes that have taken place in the past, family life will not be destroyed.

The more options available for marital and family arrangements, the greater the chance that every couple can find a happy formula for themselves. Children are serious business and once you have them, they are legally your charges, probably for at least sixteen to eighteen years, depending on the state. Marriage can be reversed, altered, or restructured. Children are not toys and cannot be returned to the store. All aspects of life have risks. Decide which ones you are willing to take.

Part IV

Finding Solutions

CHAPTER **11**

Negotiation

"How c'n I be whut I ain't? . . ."

A POWERFUL PERSON is one who can control or influence others by exercising authority. In order to gain a position of power, at least two requirements usually must be met:

1. The person who wants to be in power must possess a superior position, quality, or ability.
2. Others must recognize the person as powerful.

In a large corporation, the president may be someone clever or witty, someone who sold the most widgets, or someone who impressed the board of directors with his or her personality or intelligence. In a monarchy, the king is someone born to rule and in this case, power is simply granted. In our society, power is often bestowed because one has demonstrated superior abilities or has qualities considered socially superior. Using our present-day social standards, tell me who has more power:

—a tall or short person?
—a rich or poor person?
—an independent or a dependent?
—a more educated or a less educated person?
—a middle-class or an upper-class person?
—a physically strong or a weak person?

Women, generally, are expected to marry "up" the social scale and are shorter, poorer, more dependent, less educated, and physically weaker than their husbands. Is it surprising that women lack power in their relationships with men? A woman who married a physically smaller and weaker man with less earning power and education than herself would be in the same position as many married men—powerful. Fortunately, most people do not fall into strictly black or white categories. For example, a woman with less education than her husband may be smarter than he is regarding real estate. He seeks advice from her and is influenced by her opinion on these matters. On the other hand, she may accept his opinion when she doubts her knowledge of other subjects. For a relationship to be successful both partners must have some power. Complete domination of one partner by the other precludes any possibility of a healthy relationship. Without a position in marriage, there is no leverage for negotiation.

If you have no power in your present relationship, you can gain a position by asserting yourself. Take back your own name, create a separate bank account, recognize that your time is valuable, and get your own space. These actions will say, "Hey, I'm somebody too. I am my own person; I have my own money; I can provide services; and I have my own territory." In order to negotiate for what you want you will need a position. And most important of all, your husband

DOMINATION

NO POSITION

NEGOTIATION

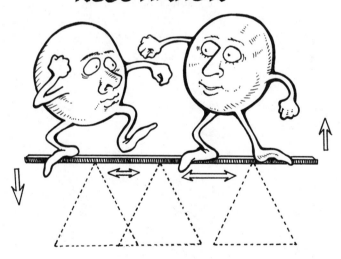

POSITION

must recognize that position. But before you can use your power, you must know what you want.

These components of the marital relationship can be considered separate entities: you, your husband, the children, and "the marriage." Before successful rules for your relationship can be formulated, concentrate on the first component—you; you must know yourself. When you and your husband each know what you want, you can negotiate about the last component—the structure of the marriage.

First, let's look at you. Do you have a position now? Do you know what changes in your life will increase your happiness? Are you negating yourself, denying what you want?

If you're not sure what will increase your marital happiness and don't know what you want, carry around a small pad for the next two weeks and jot down: (1) anything that irritates you, (2) changes you'd like to see in your relationship with your husband, and (3) the things you don't like to do and anything else you want to change. At the end of these two weeks, review your notes. Identify the two or three major recurring issues that, if resolved, will improve your life significantly. These may be small (for example, your husband always leaves an empty milk carton in the refrigerator) or large (you want to return to school).

Rules of the Game

Negotiations of any kind theoretically lead to agreements. Both sides present their views and bargain for what they want. When you married, you made an (implicit) agreement to stay together, and to love and to care for one another. If you had planned a formal wedding and your future husband wanted to wear a sports jacket, you undoubtedly discussed each point of view until an agreement was reached.

Of course, marriage can become one big compromise, leaving both partners unsatisfied—if you let it. To avoid making too many concessions, the structure of the marriage must be jockeyed until *both* partners get what they want. But there are rules to this game. Before you proceed, you and your partner should accept the conditions of a first agreement.

THE FIRST AGREEMENT

- —That you recognize that "the marriage" is an entity separate from each of you
- —That you will both seek solutions to make the marriage work
- —That you are both individuals and have rights to happiness within the marriage
- —That you agree to discuss all problems
- —That you can both present points of view, and if one partner rejects the other's point of view, it does not represent a rejection of love
- —That you will both work for the marriage and are committed to the task

The First Agreement is implicit in successful marriages and provides a foundation for negotiating all other problems.

THE STARTING LINE

Most conversations in marriage, because they reflect everyday living, are neutral or negative and task-oriented. For example:

> "Take out the garbage."
> "Have you made a dentist appointment?"
> "Did you renew the subscription?"
> "We have to go food-shopping."

It is no wonder that communication breaks down. After years of brief sentences related to daily functioning, you may believe you have nothing to say to one another.

Do you remember what you used to say on a date? Things like:

> "Did you see the movie that just opened at the Coronet?"
> "Have you ever been to Mexico? Isn't it romantic and beautiful?"
> "I like your tie. Is it silk?"

Odd as it may seem, married people need to find the time and place to converse. Often it cannot be done at home. An excellent place for conversation is a quiet and comfortable restaurant (absolutely no children allowed!). Or how about a leisurely breakfast on Sunday morning when you can both discover each other anew: What are your thoughts? What do you want out of life? What will affect your happiness? Ask these questions, and discuss business and personal problems. Discover the right setting for you and repeat this meeting whenever you feel the need to "talk." And don't wait for retirement to do it! One couple told me they finally got to talk to one another after forty years—after they both retired. They then learned things about each other that they never knew before.

SENDING SIGNALS

To complete a communication, one needs a sender and a receiver. People use a variety of wavelengths for communication. We can communicate on a spiritual plane, on an everyday stratum, and on a physical level. Ideally, we should be able to communicate with our spouses on all these levels. However, in many relationships, one or two may be lacking.

You can probably recall men who aroused you physically and met your emotional needs, but who were hard to live with on a day-to-day basis. Or men who were perfect in every way except that the chemistry between you and them was lacking. If you and your husband seem to be physically compatible and understand each other on a "day-to-day people and events" conversational level, but he does not understand your philosophical or abstract ideas, do not attempt to communicate what you want as a philosophical issue. Send your message on a wavelength that he can receive.

How You Play It

Some issues between couples can be easily solved by small structural changes in the marriage; other issues may involve considerable deliberation.

A friend complained that her husband was a gourmet cook and loved to give elaborate dinner parties. She hated to invite anyone over for dinner because it was made into a "big production"—days of preparation, not to mention the expense. Locked into the belief that they had to operate as a united front, they argued about how to entertain their friends.

I suggested that they examine the structure of their marriage and try to find a solution that would make them both happy. They did, and this is the agreement they reached: When he wanted to entertain, he would "invite" her to attend his formal fête. He would assume all costs and responsibility but she would become a willing assistant. By the same token, she could "invite" him to her informal dinner parties—taking responsibility for costs and preparation—and he would willingly assist her in the tasks she designated.

She identified what she wanted. He identified what he wanted. By keeping their money separate and assuming responsibility for what each one wanted, they eliminated an unsatisfying compromise solution. They both got what they wanted.

Fine, but what happens when you reach an impasse?

Let's say you discover that what you enjoy most is business

travel, but your husband wants you to stay home. Question each other and find out why you like to travel and why he likes you at home. Is he insecure or not trusting? Does he get lonely? Does he fear for your well-being? Do you enjoy travel because it gives you an ego boost? Or do you like to travel because it brings a new perspective? Discuss the "whys."

You will discover that fear is often at the base of most impasses. Try to identify the fear. Then—accept it. Do not try to change your partner. However, after the discussion, the anxiety may be relieved and a solution may be readily available. For example, if, in the situation described above, your husband's major objection to your travel is based on a fear of loneliness, you could try telephoning him each evening while you are out of town.

DIFFICULT PASSES

The kind of problem not easily solved by changing the structure of the marriage is represented by the following:

Lola is an attractive young woman in her thirties who married at nineteen and has yet to experience a sexual climax or any sexual satisfaction. Her husband Pete wants to be a "swinger." He believes that swapping bed partners will keep their marriage alive, but Lola won't participate. Pete doesn't know that Lola is sexually unsatisfied, and Lola was deeply hurt when Pete suggested swinging. The problem: Pete doesn't know how to satisfy Lola. Lola thinks Pete is interested in other women. The solution: Lola must communicate to Pete how he can satisfy her. Pete must reach a mutual understanding with Lola about his desire to swing.

THE GOAL POST

Someone once said, "If your sex life is good, it's only five percent of the marriage; but if it's bad, it's ninety-five percent." Sex, like housework and money, is a part of the marital relationship subject to negotiation. There are many women who don't know if they have or have not experienced a climax. Lola does not stand alone. The first rule of negotiation holds: Know yourself. Before Lola can negotiate with Pete she must know what she wants. After experimenting with herself, she may discover how her body reacts and how much time she needs to reach a state of sexual satisfaction.

Lola must decide upon her own goals for sex. Is the "climax" to be her goal? Would one satisfying two-hour session of lovemaking a month be worth more to her than three five-minute encounters a week? How interested is she in sex? She must know. Her next step is to talk to Pete.

THE MEET

The way a problem is discussed will affect its solution.

Lola decides that the bedroom is not the place to bring up their sexual problem (she is right!) and suggests to Pete that they go out alone for dinner. Pete agrees and after some discussion about property taxes getting higher, Lola changes the subject.

"Pete, I've got to talk to you about something. You want to make me happy, don't you?"

"Yes."

"Well, I think I need more time with you when we're in bed. I've just realized that we're going at it too quickly."

"Is this a reaction to my idea about the swinging?"

"No, but we should probably talk about that, too. I don't understand it. Why do you want to?"

"I don't know. I thought it would stimulate things between us."

"You mean you thought it would do *us* some good?"

"Yes. Patty and Mike said it added new life—"

"Well, I couldn't handle that. I'd rather you and I stick with each other. Are you interested in other women?"

"No."

"I've got to ask something of you, Pete."

"Sure."

"Can we agree that if either one of us decides to swing or anything else like that, that we discuss it first? I couldn't emotionally handle a surprise like that."

"That seems fair. I wouldn't have, anyway, unless you went along with it."

"I love you."

"And you worry too much."

The next time Lola and Pete are in bed making love, Lola guides Pete. They agree that there will be more time for foreplay and that he will not penetrate her until she is ready. Both Lola and Pete must keep their part of the agreement. Pete waits for her cue.

This love story has the promise of a happy ending. But what happens if Pete insists he *must* swing?

I know one woman whose husband insisted that he must have other women in his life. She thought it over. They were able to structure an agreement.

Since they both travel extensively and often meet attractive people, they came to an agreement. In essence, each said: "Your sexual relations with others are O.K., but don't tell me about it."

I remember seeing the woman in New York pursuing some of my single male friends. She told me she was very happy, very free, and that she had no intention of leaving her husband.

However, not everyone is emotionally constituted this way. (I, for one, could not subscribe to their agreement.) You must know yourself and—most important—what is emotionally acceptable to you. On an abstract level, I could understand this arrangement. For myself—never.

In fact, rarely can a marriage tolerate extramarital liaisons. If Pete insists on a "swinging" life and Lola, in truth, cannot emotionally accept the idea, the marriage is on the line. She must face Pete squarely and say "no." Because we, society, place great significance on sexual relations, tremendous hurt and misunderstanding can result from the careless encounter. For these reasons, there must be a rule, an understanding, or an agreement between partners regarding sexual relations with others. Your rule may be a simple one: "If you think about wanting someone else, let me know first."

THE PENALTY

Lola decides that she cannot stay married to a "swinging" Pete. He tells her that he knows he's a fool and maybe he'll be sorry later, but he has to experiment. Lola knows she does not want to torture herself by watching him. They decide to separate for a three-month period. During this time Lola is broken-hearted, but she knows she made the right decision for herself. Pete also made the right decision for himself. He discovers that he wants no deep commitments.

This is the so-called unhappy ending to our story, but it is much better than an ending where Lola finds a motel key in her husband's coat pocket and plays the role of the wronged woman—becoming increasingly desperate and despondent.

When you can talk through problems, you both have a chance to resolve the conflict. And if you can't resolve the issue because it means denying something integral to your happiness and well-being, you have the option of ending the relationship with dignity. Recognize what is true for you. Make the point with your partner. Establish rules you can both accept. And don't agree to anything that ultimately will destroy your potential for a happy marriage. You are responsible for your own happiness.

PUT-DOWNS

Some marriage counsellors say that arguments are healthy for marital relationships. How well you argue when you do argue may be one of the factors important to successful marriage. When you argue, be wary of put-downs and personal assaults. Stay on the subject if you can, and avoid an emotional attack on your partner's psyche.

For example, if your husband is threatened by your assertiveness, he may project his own fears by discounting your argument and saying, "I can't discuss this with you. All women are illogical." What he is really saying is: "I am not a woman. I am logical." He is afraid that *he* isn't being logical and wants to assure himself of a dominant position. Do not allow him to get away with this kind of remark. Learn to confront him by calmly stating: "What you said bothers me. I'd like to discuss it. How are all women illogical?" Do not argue your position that women are logical. Instead, ask him to explain himself until he withdraws the assault. He will probably say: "All right. All women aren't illogical." This is the time to bring the argument back to civilized discussion. Do not be intimidated. Keep your cool. Practice.

Here is another example of a put-down that I experienced with a male friend who I know has difficulty relating to women. I was walking to the grocery store when I met Stan. We exchanged "hellos" and then he asked me, "Did you see that horrible painting featured at the Holdenmeyer Gallery?"

"Yes, I went to the opening. I didn't think it was that bad."

He replied, "It, no doubt, is your taste."

I didn't react immediately, but I knew something had happened because one minute later I was angry. I thought: How dare he say that? What right does he have to judge *my* taste? I became furious. I was put down! How should I have handled this put-down? The best way is not to let the remark pass. That means being alert. Confront your opponent. To go back to my conversation with Stan—when he put me down by saying, "It, no doubt, is your taste," I should have said: "What do you mean by that?" The remaining conversation probably would have gone something like this:

"Well, you go for things no one else likes."

"And that is bad?"

(He is now on the defensive.) "Well—er—different strokes for different folks."

"I'd say so!"

The situation has been turned around. The key to eliminating the put-down from your life is to confront your opponent. Ask questions. Put him or her on the spot. I know it is easier said than done, but with practice you will learn. If someone says something that bothers you and you don't know why, say: "What you said bothers me. I'd like to discuss it." Fewer and fewer people will attempt to put you down.

WINNING POINTS

Negotiation is a continual and changing process. New ideas and approaches must be considered and slowly adopted. Don't try to do everything at once. Seemingly good old solutions will be revised and often you will search only to find there is no one right answer. In summary, these are the steps to follow for negotiating the things you want:

1. *Know yourself.*
2. Identify *what you want.*
3. Select a time and place for *discussion.*
4. *Communicate* your feelings.
5. *Create solutions.*
6. Reach an *agreement.*

7. *Test* solutions.
8. *Re-negotiate*, if necessary.

Knowing what you want and being committed to the marriage, you will find solutions. Keep your love at the base.

BE A TEAM PLAYER

All negotiations should conclude with either a written or verbal agreement. This agreement is based on *trust*.

What is trust? It is your firm belief and confidence in your partner's honesty and reliability. Agreements are meaningless unless you believe in the goodwill of your partner. Some people may say, "Well, if you *really* trusted your partner, there would be no need for any agreement." On the contrary, you can only enter into an agreement if you trust your partner. When the agreement is broken, it means that that trust has been violated. And violations of trust are what keeps lawyers busy.

Your partner should be "on your side" in front of others, even if you differ in private. I remember one man who was married to a woman of whom his family disapproved. Whenever his family was present, he would side with his parents against her. The wife felt stranded and hurt. Two years later they divorced.

Identify when it is necessary to give psychological support to your partner, even if you do not agree with what he or she is doing. For example, my husband loves to race motorcycles. In principle, I'm against motorcycles and I think racing is dangerous. But because it is important to him, I support him psychologically. When others point out the dangers of the sport and try to dissuade him from continuing with it, I do not join the bandwagon and force him into a corner. I defend his right to do what pleases him.

Use your judgment to determine when your partner needs

your help. These small considerations will help build the trust needed for future negotiations and agreements.

Without rules in the game of marriage, problems are more likely to occur because relationship boundaries are vague. As equal partners in the marriage, you both can negotiate for the things you want.

CHAPTER 12

Troubles with Tigers

"Though I can feel the undertow, I never make a complaint...."

THE EXPERIMENTS IN THIS BOOK are recommended on the assumption that your partner is a normal, healthy, and reasonably secure male who has not questioned his role as husband and provider. Most of the time your man is probably agreeable, although he may be resistant to new ideas, new concepts, and change. That's normal. However, there are men who are not normal—they may be severely insecure or mentally sick. Although ways to achieve happiness in marriage are suggested in this book, there are special situations for which the best or only solution may be to walk away.

Stalking the Wildcat

Before you launch a campaign to reexamine and change the structure of your marriage, decide if your present relationship is capable of bearing the stress that change may bring and if your love for one another is worth keeping. Some men may not permit happiness under any type of marital arrangement. If you are married to such a man, there is very little you can do to change the quality of your married life. The insecure man will be threatened and the psychologically disturbed man may attempt to harm you physically. These men need professional help that you cannot easily provide. For any approach to marital happiness to succeed, you must both share the desire to work for it. And you both must be psychologically capable of allowing happiness to enter your life. Recognize the man (or woman) unable to commit himself to loving you—not because you are unlovable but because he is deeply troubled. Recognize the man who doesn't care—not because you are unworthy but because he is incorrigible.

There are men who create problems for women just as there are women who create problems for men. In this chapter, only a few troubled situations are described. Depending on the severity of the problem and the damage to the relationship, a situation can be either difficult or impossible to improve. Restructuring your marriage can often help the difficult situation but will probably not correct the impossible one.

DOMESTIC DIFFICULTIES

The Immature Cat: A woman, unhappy with her marriage, explained her situation to me: Her husband is unemployed and she works. They have no children. When she returns from her job she usually finds him planted in front of the television set, feet skyward, in his favorite reclining chair. She enters the room; he doesn't say hello. She prepares dinner every night and cleans the house. But what really disturbs her is the fact that he recently purchased a four-wheel-drive pickup truck with the money she hoped would finance the down payment on a house. His new "toy" was purchased with her earnings. Married in her teens, she is afraid of divorce. She loves him. Inadvertently, she contributes to his immaturity. Playing mother to her man keeps him a child. Restructuring their marriage might help him to grow and assume responsibility, especially if they were to adopt the Separate Property System.

The Insecure Cat: Your tiger can be sexually insecure, afraid of responsibility, or a combination of these and other shortcomings. He depends on you. He also demands your attention and love. He is easily upset if you assert yourself, yet he wants you to be his Rock of Gibraltar. Restructuring the marriage may help the insecure man to grow psychologically, but if he is severely threatened by your assertiveness, any suggestion of modifying his position of control will send him into a tailspin. He wants you safely under this thumb, which he considers *your place.* He would be lost without you.

If you are married to an immature or insecure man, try the restructuring techniques described in the previous chapters. Restructuring the marriage may provide a healthy challenge to the relationship and promote mutual growth.

The Cheetah: Most love relationships are possessive. Denying this fact may be a means of fooling yourself. Feelings of jealousy arise from the desire to possess your lover. The response is perfectly natural. For this reason, the discovered extramarital relationship can arouse intense wrath.

Except for the rare couple who can honestly permit sexual exploration with others, extramarital affairs can permanently damage your love relationship with your mate. If you are married to a cheating man, it is very difficult, although not always impossible, to restructure away the hurt. Marriage is based on love and trust. The base of your marriage will be shaky until trust can be reestablished. Determine if you are capable of forgiving and forgetting and if he is willing to agree to a policy of honesty. Design the structure of your new relationship, starting without preconceived notions. Your new independence just may spark interest in the affair at home.

The Impossible Situation: A Tiger Cage

Our society defines men as "tough." Women sometimes confuse this concept of masculinity with idealized sexual relations. If he treats you rough, he's a man—that makes you more of a (submissive) woman. Present law, based on English common law, according to which the wife is considered property, does not alleviate the problem. By tradition, a wife is bound to have sexual relations with her husband on demand.

In the cool judgment of right-thinking women, compulsory sexual intercourse is not a husband's right in marriage, for such a "right" gives the lie to any concept of equality and human dignity. Consent is better arrived at by husband and wife afresh each time, for if women are to be what we believe we are—equal partners—then intercourse must be construed as an act of mutual desire and not as a wifely "duty" enforced by the permissible threat of bodily harm or of economic sanctions.*

My husband and I were living in a small apartment building in Oakland, California. I was sitting in a lounge chair on the tenants' patio one day when a young woman about eighteen years old sat down in the chair beside me. She was a little plump, not unattractive, just married, and very talkative. She told me proudly that she was the first one in her high school class to get married. Her husband came from the same small town in Pennsylvania as she did and had been stationed at a nearby navy base. They were only married two months when he was called for sea duty and so they moved from Pennsylvania to California, where she knew no one. She talked about her marriage and about how disappointed her

* Susan Brownmiller, *Against Our Will: Men, Women and Rape* (New York: Simon and Schuster, 1975), p. 381.

family and her husband were because she was not pregnant. I asked her why she wanted to get pregnant so soon. She replied that everyone wanted her to have a baby. And naturally she wanted to please her husband and everyone else. Finally she confided that she wasn't sure that she wanted a child. I suggested that she get some form of birth control until she was sure and not to worry about it.

Her husband came home on leave for about two weeks and then left for Japan. I saw her again on the patio. Looking very unhappy and lonely, she asked me if I knew how to get a divorce. I was surprised. I could not imagine what could have happened in two weeks. She told me her sad story.

She was a virgin before she married and was raped during her honeymoon. ("Rape" means forced sexual intercourse under psychological or physical duress.) She said she refused his advances because she had her "period," but he was drunk, assaulted her, and penetrated her forcibly. Several days later she was hospitalized and received several stitches for vaginal lacerations. Her disillusionment was profound, but she was too embarrassed to tell anyone. When he returned on his two-week shore leave, he again abused her, this time leaving her with another reminder of him—a case of gonorrhea. She went to a clinic and received immediate treatment. She asked me if I thought becoming pregnant would help her marriage. I told her that it probably would not help. I gave her the encouragement she needed to get a divorce and to ask for her own name back. She was bitter, angry, and hurt, but delighted to discover his name did not have to be carried by her for the ensuing years. She filed for divorce and returned to Pennsylvania to live with her parents. She wrote to me shortly thereafter. She was happy, pursuing a nursing career. Her ex-husband, the last I heard, was living with a woman he met in Japan.

This man, in my opinion, was mentally sick. The woman was young, perhaps immature, but she was not a psychological misfit. Leaving him was the appropriate thing to do. Any attempts to restructure their marriage would not have worked.

In many seemingly impossible situations there are enough good times to make the horrible scenes bearable. One night, while I was living in Boston, I heard the screams of a young woman as she was kicked and punched down a stairwell. With a surge of bravado I rescued the damsel in distress. I locked her in my apartment and nursed her wounds; she had a broken thumb. Her husband—a handsome fellow—paced the hallway waiting for his prey while threatening to kill *me*. I called the police. When the officers arrived, the wife refused to press charges. The police were familiar with the couple's case. The previous summer her husband had stuffed rags down her throat.

She told me she couldn't leave him. Where could she go? I offered her the money to go back to Florida, where she had friends. She stayed the night in my apartment to think it over. The next morning I left for work, and when I returned, she was gone. She and her husband were back together again. They simply kissed and made up. Was she happy? Was he? I don't know.

She had asked me if I thought she was a masochist and he a sadist, or if maybe their violence was due to hostile sexual feelings from a rigid Catholic upbringing, or if she was wrong to stay with him because even though he was cruel, she knew he loved her.

If you find yourself in an impossible situation, you must face your life squarely. Are you taking abuse from your man? Do you want to be a victim? Are you prepared to leave? If you feel "he needs me," you are in a trap. Some men who "need you" may be surviving quite well while you pay the price for their hang-ups or their bad childhood experiences with their mothers. If you are willing to stay and suffer, your deranged man will provide the cruel action. If you enjoy rough treatment, then *you* are the one who needs psychological counselling. To leave a man who "needs you" is difficult, especially when at times he meets some of your needs, too, and occasionally brings you happiness. If you leave him, you will face lonely nights. You will miss the good times and forget his cruelty. If you decide to leave him, take with you the memory of his worst offense. Every time you consider going back—recall that worst memory. Love yourself as he cannot love you.

Recognize when a situation is impossible. A man who beats you, who forces intercourse, who is constantly drunk, who demands children or rejects them, or who flaunts other women in your face is a sick man. He may "need" you to torture, but you do not need him. Get out! If you love yourself, you will not spend your short life trying to salvage the abusive man. Even if you "cure" him, he may thank you kindly, go on his way, and seek to establish himself in a new relationship.

This book is not a vehicle to happiness for an impossible relationship. The techniques suggested here will be valuable for average folk who have not severely wounded their relationships with extramarital affairs, dishonesty, and unusual cruelty. If your husband needs professional help or if you have been very hurt, following the principles in this book may not save the marriage, but they will better prepare you to take action on your own behalf. You will be free. You may be in the cage, but you won't be trapped.

Part V

Starting from Home Base

CHAPTER 13

Keystones

"I only did the kind of things I oughta, sorta. . . ."

PERHAPS YOU AGREE that the suggestions given in this book are good ideas based on a philosophy of equality and fair play, but, when viewing your own situation, you are hesitant to adopt such a partnership. In this chapter we will discuss the requisites for a happy marriage and raise important questions. We will evaluate where *you* stand.

Requisites

Liking is an important part of any relationship and essential to love. Do you like your partner? Does he or she have the qualities you admire in a person? Also essential is the presence of a hard-to-define attraction called body chemistry. Physical attraction is often so powerful that people with few other interests or values in common can live together on chemical reactions alone.

ORGANIC CHEMISTRY

Common values and shared interests are nice to have between people but they are not necessary for happy marriage. If you subscribe to a marital philosophy based on a husband and wife sharing all aspects of their lives and doing everything together, then mutual happiness would demand that you and your partner both be alike in as many ways as possible. If you subscribe to the marital philosophy promoted in this book—that each partner has a separate identity and needs space—then fewer requirements are needed for happiness in marriage. But regardless of your philosophy, physical attraction is requisite to a successful, vibrant marriage. Usually, these vibrations precede love. You must like each other *physically* for the marriage to endure. And that physical attraction does not depend on clothes, hairstyle, or makeup.

Are you both as physically healthy as you were when you met? Do you care enough about yourselves to stay in shape? How you look does affect attractiveness, but it is not the sole element. A physical presence that says, "I love myself, I take care of myself" attracts.

What is your answer to this question: Are you and your partner physically drawn to each other?

If you answered "yes," you have one requirement for a successful marriage and a wonderful chance to work toward other kinds of fulfillment in your marriage. But if you find yourself no longer physically attracted to your partner, determine if some physical change has taken place that has "turned you off." If you discover it's your husband's pot belly that you dislike, don't criticize him or his looks. If you want the marriage to continue, but you want the spark back, adopt the suggestions for independence given in this book. After all, if you're free of economic dependencies, all that remains to hold you together is love. Your husband will probably start to take stock of himself. Love can foster physical attraction, and physical attractiveness can give love a boost.

BASIC BIOLOGY

In marriage physical communication other than sex is another essential to success. This interchange usually starts with touching. Most normal living beings love to be handled, touched, petted, and even playfully poked. Human beings need to be touched on a regular basis. Is there a better way to say "I love you" than to embrace afresh each time you meet? For many people the desire to hold and to be held is naturally evident and practiced. For others, any physical embrace means "we're going to bed."

Touching and embracing are more important to our mental health than sex. Our society worships the Sex God but our need for intercourse follows our need for air, water, food, and tactile stimulation.

Marriage does not mean that you own your partner sexually or otherwise. Just as when you were single, physical intimacies should be shared at the height of physical desire. Be sure that you are *both* eager (even if it takes weeks or months to feel that way) when you engage in sexual relations. Enjoy the desire. When the urge hits you both—be it in the morning, afternoon, or evening; in the dining room, bedroom, or parlor—take your time to relish it, to luxuriate in the splendor. Nothing will kill your romance faster than sex on demand or making love to fill a 2.5 weekly average.

SOCIOBIOLOGY ASSIGNMENT:

To help free yourselves of set social roles and to put new life into your sexual play, vary your routine occasionally. For example, if you are usually passive, become the aggressive female who attracts and seduces her husband—then play the dominant sex role in bed. Trading the usual roles can be fun. It will also increase awareness of the impact of social conditioning.

Expectations

Wrapped up in marriage are the social expectations of others. Wrapped up in ourselves are the expectations we have of our spouse. Romantic expectations are often unrealistic. Your husband is only a human being. Like mine, he may appear to have been born with **Original Fault.**

GEOLOGY: ORIGINAL FAULT

This condition is peculiar to marital partners. Whenever things go wrong, it is the other's fault. "If it hadn't been for you—" is the common cry of the person married to a partner with Original Fault. No one person can reasonably satisfy all your expectations. Occasionally, you will be disappointed because your partner did not meet you halfway or even try. You may also be disappointed in yourself for not achieving the marital picture you had in mind. One can punish his or her partner and oneself for not meeting expectations. But who set the goals?

When my husband disappoints me, I can usually trace my expectations back to my parents' home. My husband is not my mother or my father. When I was sick, he was a lousy nurse. When I needed advice, he failed to counsel. Can I expect him to nurture me like my mother or to be a guardian like my father? I can only expect him to be himself. In other ways, he has exceeded my expectations. He is handy around the house. I never expect him to be on time and he is always on time. He calls if he is going to be late. He does what he says he is going to do. He is tender and loving. But still he does not meet *all* my needs.

BRIDGING THE GAPS

It is unreasonable to expect one person to satisfy you in every area. If he or she does, fantastic! If he or she does not, there is no reason to be alarmed. Fortunately, friendships are available outside marriage. Be happy with what you have, with what works, inside the marriage.

Cyra is an attractive secretary for a large firm. Her husband is a contractor. She is intrigued by Eastern religions, but can't interest her husband in the topic. She meets Bruce, an expert on religions of the world. He is dashing and exciting and asks Cyra to meet him for a drink after work. Cyra wants to get to know Bruce but is afraid. What should she do?

If she and her husband have established rules for their relationship she will know where to "draw the line" with men other than her husband. Most marriages can successfully tolerate any "arm's-length" relationship with others. Bruce is meeting Cyra's need for stimulating conversation on a subject of special interest. If she has a marriage based on love and trust, she should be able to tell her husband that she wants to discuss world religions with Bruce. (Her husband should be free to join them if he wishes.) While she is with Bruce, she should enjoy herself fully, letting Bruce know the rules of her game in case there is any question.

If she finds herself very attracted to him physically as well, she must weigh the risks: What does she have to lose? What does she gain?

When you have something to lose, you will not want to take any risks. Relationships with other men can be enjoyable and rewarding because they meet a particular need. Cherish them and keep the friends on whom you can rely.

You need others in your life outside the marriage to keep your balance. If my husband cannot be sympathetic, I can always talk to my sister. If he can't give me counsel, I can talk to my friend Hank. If my husband's not willing to listen to my ideas, my friend Fay will understand. Friends augment happiness. I appreciate and love them. Since I am responsible for my own happiness, I make an effort to satisfy through others what can't be satisfied within my marital relationship. My needs will change, my husband's responses to my needs will change, and our relationship will change. We need others to balance our lives and to complement the marriage as it matures.

Buttes and Rebuttals

A partnership implies that two or more people have an agreement to work together toward a common goal. A realistic expectation of the marriage should be that you both share the same goal: happiness and freedom in marriage. Your expectations are key to whether you will find this happiness. If you expect your partner to be all things, you can expect disappointment on a regular basis. Accept him as he is. Similarly, he should accept you as you are. Any changes in your relationship to meet unsatisfied expectations can either be negotiated or sought outside the marriage.

For example, my husband dislikes parties. I've tried for years to negotiate an agreement with him, since I want to go to parties and would like him to come along. We were unsuccessful in finding a solution that would guarantee his accompanying me. I had a choice: I could stay home with him or go to parties without him.

As a result, we incorporated the Right of First Refusal into our relationship.

THE RIGHT OF FIRST REFUSAL:

This means that each partner will give the other an opportunity to share in every undertaking. But if one partner isn't interested, the other is free to engage others. In other words, if your partner says "no" to an invitation, you are free to ask someone else or go by yourself.

When we get a party invitation, I ask my husband if he's going. If he doesn't want to go, I usually go by myself and when asked the whereabouts of my husband by the hostess, I tell the truth: "Fred wanted to get some work done to-night," or "Fred wanted to rest tonight, but says 'hello.'" If the occasion requires a partner and we are invited to come "together," I may be out of luck. Depending on the situation and the flexibility of the hosts, I can again opt to go by myself or enlist another partner for the evening.

In the beginning, I felt awkward going to events "un-coupled." Then I discovered that the party experience varied according to whether I was by myself or with my husband. By myself, I met more people and had involved conversa-tions. With my husband, we tended to spend the time talking together, thus learning more about one another, and only occasionally branching out to meet others. Both party experi-ences are enjoyable, but they are different.

Always give your partner the Right of First Refusal. *Not* asking your partner to go some place (even if you know he'd rather stay home) can hurt. My husband asked me to join him on his trip to Alaska. I didn't want to go. If he had announced he was going without me, I would have been upset. Since he asked me, I felt loved and happy to see him on his own.

THE WOBBLE

Throughout our lifetimes we make decisions. A marriage that puts the individual ahead of the unit has been outlined in this book. Is it for you?

I met a charming woman, one about to get married, who asserted that she definitely wanted to keep her own name and have her own money, but her future husband was very rich and she wanted him to support her. I laughed. I don't blame her for wanting to have her cake and eat it too. If she kept a reserve of money, she would not be totally dependent on her husband. But if he is supporting her, she is not standing on her own two feet. She would be in a compromised position. Her decision: Shall it be her own limited money with independence and freedom, or access to his fortune with dependence and obligation?

When the incomes of two partners are extremely disproportionate, it is tempting to opt for the joint shared account because the poorer partner thinks he or she gets a better deal. Take this situation: You are a research assistant who makes $4,000 a year. You marry a millionaire. What should you do? The answer to this question depends on the answers to other questions.

Do you want complete independence and freedom?

Is freedom the key to your happiness?

Do you want equal power in your relationship with your husband?

Do you care enough to want to maintain the relationship?

If you answered "yes" to all four questions, keep your money separate and follow the suggestions in this book. Your millionaire husband can buy a house as his separate property and anything else he wants. If you want to own part of the mansion he buys, contribute what you can afford—even if it is only one percent—but as your separate property. He is free to buy what he wishes and you undoubtedly will benefit from some of his purchases. If he wishes you to own them, he can present them to you as gifts or leave them to you in his will. You can both maintain sovereignty.

The decision to provide for yourself, to carry your own weight in a relationship, is difficult if you are not able to provide as well for yourself as you could by sharing all income. Only after you evaluate the importance of your own freedom and determine whether your happiness is dependent on that freedom will you be able to make this decision. (Review the advice given in Chapter 3 again.)

Major arguments in support of the notion that you have no choice are "the Rich Argument," "the Poor Argument," and "the Selfish Argument," explained in the following paragraphs. These arguments are excuses for staying locked into mutually dependent and unfree relationships.

THE RICH ARGUMENT:

"I really want independence but my husband makes so much money that it makes no sense for me to work. It would just put us in a higher tax bracket and my earnings hardly would contribute anything."

If you follow the recommendations given in Chapter 7, the Rich Argument will not hold. You can separate your property—that means earned income too—and file separate tax returns. Your earnings, if filed "married, filing separately," will not add to your husband's income; but he will lose a deduction, since you are no longer a dependent (a loss of one exemption). Also, generally, at the same income level with the same number of exemptions the tax rate is higher for "married, filing separately" than "married, filing joint return" (an inequity in the law). This puts him in a higher tax bracket, but it puts you in a better bargaining position. Unless he is in a 100-percent tax bracket (which is impossible), your income still adds to the till for joint purchases. If you are a homemaker and he pays you, you can (for tax purposes) be considered a dependent, even though you use the Separate Property System. If desired, the homemaker could become an employee, in which case her income is taxed and her husband subject to laws pertaining to employers. But I see no financial advantage to this latter arrangement. If filing a joint tax return instead of separate returns will save you both some money (which it usually does), your husband will then welcome your added earnings.

"Everything that you suggest in this book assumes that people have money. All the money we have goes into one pot just to pay the bills. When you're in debt, it doesn't matter who earns the money."

The Poor Argument suggests that two live more expensively together than apart. For some couples this may be true. Separate your money and divide the responsibility for the bills. If your partner can't pay his fair share, loan him the money. If you follow the Separate Property System, "joint" purchases will be identified. (Do not pay for expenses unless you have agreed to pay for them.)

Another version of the Poor Argument goes like this: "What you're suggesting is good only for the middle class. Many women have to pay the bills because their men are unemployed."

This argument also suggests that a couple must operate as a unit. If your husband has a small income or is unemployed, you can still use the Separate Property System. A woman complained to me that her fiance didn't make as much money as she did, and that if she supported him, he would lose his dignity. They feared marriage because of his predicament. I suggested they adopt the Separate Property System. He could pay his fair share of the living costs, which should be less than if he were living alone. She could buy herself whatever she wanted. If she did not give him handouts, he could retain his dignity. The idea gave them a new lease on their relationship, which previously they had considered unworkable because her income was so much larger than his. When you pay your own way, you maintain not only your freedom but your dignity as well.

THE SELFISH ARGUMENT:

"Yes, but what you are suggesting is selfish."

Selfish! If you get pleasure, if you are happy, if you do what you want to do, others may call you selfish.

Being *for yourself* and being selfish are not to be confused.

Webster's Dictionary defines "selfish" as "having such regard for one's own interests and advantage that the welfare of others becomes of less concern than is considered just" or "caring unduly or supremely for oneself; regarding one's own comfort, advantage, etc. *in disregard* or *at the expense, of others.*"

Being for yourself can be defined as having an appreciation of one's own interests, the desire to actualize happiness for oneself in harmony with others—in high regard for, and *not* at the expense of, the self-interest of others.

In contrast, I offer an example of not being for yourself. On the early morning news, the radio broadcaster announced: ". . . woman in her mid-twenties jumped off the bridge ninety minutes ago. The Coast Guard is returning her unidentified body. A note found in her car said, 'I couldn't live without you.'"

A broken heart caused this woman in her twenties to leap to her death. Was her lover a rotten man? Or was her self-love so low that rejection was too hard to bear? People end their own lives because the pain of living is so great. Suicide is a way to alleviate the pain and to cause hurt to others.

I once asked my husband what he would do if I left him. He said, "I'd realize that you had poor judgment."

I was amazed! God bless his wonderful, highly developed male ego. My answer, if he'd asked the question of me, would have been, "I would wonder what I did wrong." Note what, in essence, we each said:

He said: I'm wonderful, therefore any rejection of me by someone else is his or her failure to see me in my true light.

I said: I'm probably not wonderful, therefore any rejection by someone else confirms that I lack something.

Realizing that his attitude is a marvelous defense against the hurt of rejection, I encourage everyone to adopt a similar posture. No love relationship should ever become so important that you physically or psychologically sacrifice yourself. (I know that's easier to say than to follow.)

Love yourself first and then allow others to love you. Paradoxically, by loving yourself you are also better able to love others. If you lose the person you want (especially to another), remember that his disaffection does not reflect your value but does reflect his taste. There is no *one* right person. You always will have yourself and that is worth preserving. You are valuable. There is no virtue in being self-less.

A Practicum

Sometimes decisions are hard to make. You may ask yourself: How do I know what I want? How will I know if I want all this independence?

One very simple technique that has always worked for me is the "Flip-a-Coin Test."

For example, let's assume you must make a career decision that involves a new location. The new location is less desirable than your present one, but the job is better. How will you decide?

Clear your mind as best you can of all thoughts, in order to discover how you *really feel*. Make believe that whatever the toss of the coin predicts is what will happen. Heads, for instance, will mean that you stay in your present job. Tails will mean that you take the better job in the less desirable location. Flip the coin. Slap it on your hand and look. What was it? Heads or tails? What was your reaction? If your immediate reaction was a feeling of joy—that's what you want. If you felt uncertain or disappointed—that's the road you don't want to take.

Early in my marriage, when I was trying to decide whether or not to use my own name, I was in conflict. On the one hand, I wanted to use my own name; but on the other hand, I wanted to show our cohesiveness by assuming my husband's name. I took the Flip-a-Coin Test and every time heads (keeping my own name) came up, I felt happy. Every time tails (assuming his name) came up, I was disappointed and wanted to do the test over again. It was clear what I really wanted.

UNWRITTEN RULES

Over the years, almost unconsciously, my husband and I have developed a working set of rules to govern our life together. Every couple should create the working rules of their own relationship. Remember, there are always exceptions to rules, and rules can be changed through negotiation.

Our working set of rules is presented, not as a guide appropriate for everyone, but as an example of one couple's living arrangement. We generally adhere to the following notions:

On money: We keep our money separate (separate savings and checking accounts) and we bill each other monthly for joint expenses. We have agreed to loan each other money if necessity dictates.

On sex: Our sexual relationship is based on mutual desire. Extramarital liaisons are not tolerated. But, if forewarned, we have agreed, one partner has a difficult decision to make—to stay or go. We would then both know what to expect. Sex is never to be used as a negotiating tool.

On identity: We use our given names.

On housework: We are each in charge of specific rooms in the house. If we hire outside help, we split the cost.

On laundry: We do our own laundry and pay for our own cleaning bills.

On space: We have our own bedrooms and maintain separate offices.

On dining out: We settle the bill at the table or keep track of the expense. If the tabs are close, we may consider it a joint expense.

On children: We do not want children, but if we changed our minds we would consider adopting an older child.

On negotiation: If we each know what we want, we work toward a solution that we can both accept.

On meal preparation: I do all the cleaning up and he does all the cooking. If he comes home late, I cook and he cleans.

On parties: We are usually invited together, but I'll go by myself if he won't come.

On garbage: We both load the pail with trash from our assigned "rooms to clean." He puts it out and I take it in after the sanitation workers have emptied it.

On Christmas cards and correspondence: We each meet social obligations toward our own family and friends. The same rule applies for gifts, although the cards sent with the gifts and letters are signed from us both. Expenses are not joint.

On auto trips: We use his car; he does most of the driving. I pay for the gas and tolls.

On anything else: If there is not a rule and no problem, there is no need for a rule. If there is no rule and a problem, there will soon be a rule.

In addition, we share these attitudes about our relationship:

On living together: It has all the traps and none of the "security" of marriage. It might have been preferable for us both, but we took the conventional route.

On marriage: It is a way for us to belong to society and a very stabilizing force in our lives.

On contracts: The contract is a way for us to regulate our relationship without involving society.

On romance: We believe independence fosters love.

On love: We have it and we let each other know it *often.*

These rules (and beliefs) have never been written into con-tract form. They exist because over the years—not in one day —we discovered that this pattern of organization enabled us to achieve increased happiness in our marriage.

Free people are happy people. Love will support a marriage between individuals. Mutual respect, seasoned with an under-standing of the feelings you share, is a goal worthy of the effort.

The key to a happy and healthy relationship will differ for each couple. When you find the key to your happiness, resist any temptation to relinquish it. If a relationship has been troubled, accept the prospect of change. Relationships can be happy and you can be happy continuously. It's all right to have a good relationship. It's all right to have a relationship without extreme highs and lows. It's all right to have one with highs and lows. It's all right to be happy. The choice is yours. Give yourself permission.

CHAPTER **14**

Doing It

"Whut you goin' to do when he talks thet way? Spit in his eye? ..."

ONCE YOU TAKE BACK YOUR OWN NAME, separate your money, meditate in your own room, and divide household responsibilities, your marriage may start to look like divorce. Structuring your marriage to eliminate economic dependency does make divorce easier, but it also makes a happier marriage possible, thereby decreasing the likelihood of a split. Your marriage will be bonded by one thing—your feelings for each other.

Why, you may ask, be legally married? Why not just live together?

In and Out of Marriage

Romantic relationships can be categorized as either short-term or long-term. Short-term relationships may last from one day to six months. Within six months (or minutes) of knowing someone, you can probably tell whether or not the relationship has long-term potential. With any romance that has long-term implications, consideration should be given to the relationship's structure—especially if you decide to live together.

"Living together" is subject to the same traps as institutionalized marriage except that you start with different assumptions, greater insecurity, and a mind-set that limits all planning ahead.

The now-famous case of actor Lee Marvin and Michelle Triola throws into chaos many previous assumptions about partners who live together. After six years of living together, Lee and Michelle's romance ended. She claimed that she and Lee had had a verbal agreement: He had promised to support her and thus she had become a homemaker, sacrificing a budding singing career. She sued Marvin for one million dollars and the court says she has a case. Marriage and divorce lawyers don't know what to expect next. Law books may be rewritten.

Many people live together not only to test their relationships in a "trial marriage" but to avoid legal pitfalls if the "marriage" should sour. Living together, however, as the Marvin case exemplifies, does not guarantee a living arrangement free from legal obligation. For this reason, couples living together today are writing partnership agreements or contracts specifying the terms of their relationships.

If you are living together and about to be married, you may want to wait several months (until the wedding trauma is over) before you start the negotiation process. Before I married, the idea of negotiating for the kind of relationship I wanted in marriage was a foreign thought. What I wanted was him. My thoughts stopped there. In love, carried away by my emotions and impulsive, I was flying high. Marriage would be an extension of that romance. I knew only one thing: I loved him. I believed that love was all that was necessary for everlasting happiness. It was a wonderful beginning and that's the way it should be.

However, I later discovered that even with love at the base, marriage did not guarantee happiness. If anything, marriage could destroy that love. Couples who have lived together prior to marriage attest to the fact that being married changes the relationship. Before you *are* married, you cannot wisely negotiate for what you want because you don't know what the problems are. You don't know what impact the marriage will have on each of your psyches. My husband changed after marriage, as did I. He became more attentive and loving than when we were courting and I became angry because I felt social pressure to conform to a traditional married lifestyle. We surprised ourselves and considered divorce a solution, since the cause of our grief seemed to be marriage. As one man said to me, "Marriage is the biggest crap shoot in town."

After you are married—and by virtue of that fact—your relationship will change. Social expectations are likely to reveal dimensions, not previously considered, about your relationship. You will need time and the commitment marriage brings to iron out the details of your new partnership.

Determine for yourself if your relationship—or your psyche—needs marriage. I resisted marriage for many years, holding the 1950s' view that marriage would conflict with my career. At the same time, because our culture supports marriage as a goal for women, my self-worth was, in part, dependent on achieving married status.

To illustrate how strong our social need for marriage can be, let me recite one friend's experience. He had recently divorced and met an intelligent and attractive woman, a divorcée of several years, with a thirteen-year-old daughter. She fell head over heels in love with him and desperately wanted marriage. He was unsure as to whether or not he wanted to marry again, but having lost the lease on his apartment and having no place to live, he moved in with her. After several months she gave him an ultimatum: Marry me or move out. Fair enough. He asked me if I thought he should marry her. I suggested that he move out and wait until he knew what he was doing. Although I knew he enjoyed her company and received the "royal treatment" in her home, I felt he was being pushed into a permanent relationship. I was also aware that I obviously didn't know all the dimensions of their mutual attraction. I told him not to involve us further (meaning my husband and myself) in his romance. He appeared to assume an almost passive role while she eagerly pursued the goal of marriage. Finally, she went into an emotional tirade, forcing him to decide, and "won" her man.

That marriage is still a goal for many women (and for some men) cannot be denied. If we are insecure about our relationship, marriage—the goal—appears to be the solution. And, I admit, I fell for it.

Social pressure mounted as I got older. Marriage, to me, was The Great Unknown. Fearful of the consequences, I married anyway. For the sake of my psyche, I had to get married. And I was lucky. I married a marvelous and reasonable man. We were able to build a marriage that counteracted the inequities of tradition. We share a love that grows deeper and deeper every year. If we ever part, I will never regret the years we spent together. I doubt, however, that I would ever marry again. My psychological need for the state of marriage has abated. Having witnessed how marriage can destroy good relationships, I no longer *need* marriage.

Because people change and because there are many people with whom you could be happily married, all relationships have the potential for ending. Couples who have structured their marriages according to the guidelines in this book will have solutions to the pitfalls of marriage and a lease on living together.

If marriage is not essential to your psyche, forego the legal papers of the state and exchange them instead for a partnership contract. A contract between partners, renewed yearly, is my ideal of how a relationship should work. But how many of us can buck the pressure of tradition? Most of us end up married.

WRITTEN WORDS

Among the very rich, the concepts discussed in this book are hardly surprising. For centuries, the moneyed have entered into contracts before, during, and after marriage. They have maintained separate bank accounts, have had their own bedrooms or separate villas, have had others manage their domestic chores and children, and have taken separate vacations.

Pat and Richard Nixon had separate bedrooms. Jackie Onassis had a marriage contract with Ari. "According to Christian Kafarakis, former chief steward on Aristotle Onassis' yacht, the marriage contract between Onassis and Jacqueline Bouvier Kennedy contain(ed) 170 clauses, covering every possible detail of their marital life." *

Regardless of whether you are living together or married, rich or poor, if you don't set the rules of your relationship, the state will. The most important agreement to be put into writing is a contract regarding your finances. My husband and I have only one written contract and it concerns money. This contract serves two purposes: (1) it keeps money problems out of our marriage, and (2), in the event of divorce, it would keep money out of the battle.

---

* Edmiston, "How to Write Your Own Marriage Contract."

Our Separate Property Agreement

AGREEMENT

WE, ANNE MARTHA SEIFERT, and FRED H. WILLIS, husband and wife, hereby agree as follows:

(1) Each and all of the items of property, or interests therein of whatever kind and character, of each of us, shall be the separate property of the person in whose name title to that property is held, or of the person in whose possession said property is held.

(2) Each of our earnings and accumulations have been, throughout the duration of our marriage, and shall continue to be so long as we are married, the separate property of each of us, respectively.

(3) Each of us is free to manage and control his or her own property without the consent or agreement of the other party.

IN WITNESS WHEREOF, we have hereunto set our hands this 14th day of February, 1973.

_____
Anne Martha Seifert

_____
Fred H. Willis

Parting Words

To repeat, if I had to do it over again, I would not get married. There is no reason to involve the state in one's love affair. You may wonder why, if I find marriage so onerous, I am still married. My husband and I discussed living together with a partnership agreement as an alternative to marriage. But, since we are legally married, we would need to divorce in order to live together as unmarrieds. We believe we have circumvented the oppressiveness of marriage by retaining our financial independence. This book discusses that undefined area between marriage, as we commonly know it, and living together as a temporary pacifier. Maybe you can find where you stand on the couple continuum depicted below.

THE COUPLE CONTINUUM

Governed by State and Federal Law			*Governed by Common Law*		
Marriage with the Blessed Assumptions	Marriage with Role-Sharing	Marriage with the Separate Property System	Living Together with a Partnership Agreement	Living Together with a Verbal Agreement	Living Together Free and Easy

Social Oppression .... Relative Freedom

For the most part, the state is an almost silent partner during marriage but can become a strong voice in divorce. One friend, a lawyer, told me she plans to be "married" but will keep the state out of it by forgoing the marriage license. An announcement will appear in the paper and she will have a wedding with all the trimmings. She visualizes a garden ceremony, with a close friend or understanding preacher administering the vows.

Marriage, for most people, is still a desirable goal. Why? Because of its long tradition in our culture and because marriage symbolizes the sanctioning of love. Marriage is a public statement of each partner's commitment to the other. Simply stated, marriage is a milestone. Marriage is social cement.

My husband and I are aware that it would be easy for us to part whenever we desired because we are not dependent on one another for financial or social support. Yet we stay together. Our commitment is strong and we work hard to keep the relationship going.

Feeling free, love is reinforced because of the knowledge that your partner is by your side clearly by choice; it's a great compliment. You are free to love, to care, and to share. If you change your ways or your partner changes his, a marriage based on the ideals set forth in this book can flex to absorb them.

If love and a basis for caring exist, restructuring your marriage toward mutual independence will enrich the relationship. If love does not exist, restructuring your marriage in this way will bare the bones. (You may discover that *only* economic dependency has held the marriage together.)

Marriage based on dependent obligation is destructive to the core. Money often is the Number One culprit in causing marital strife. Take the money out of your marriage and make your love count again.

You can enjoy your marriage. You can be free. You can be happy. You can stand on your own two feet.

- Label your marriage so that it reflects the two independent individuals it binds. Two people, two names.
- Use the Separate Property System to remove the economic dependency of an unbalanced marriage structure.
- Assign the household chores through a negotiation process between equally powerful partners.
- If locked dependency is removed at the base, love will take its place. Get the space you need for that love to grow.

What is left of the marriage is what you started with—your happiness, your love, your independence, and the spirit that once nurtured your feelings toward one another.

Discovering the road, reading about what to do and then not doing it will keep you where you are. Do not allow the Blessed Assumptions to lead you. Do not let your marriage destroy your love. Engage in the hard work required to restructure the marriage. A happy marriage is worth the time, effort, and labor invested. You will both need courage to identify what you want and then go after it.

I wish you a freedom few married couples experience. You have the key to independence and happiness in marriage.

Now open the door.